Always on Lockdown

An Oral History of Policing and
Discipline Inside Public Schools

Horace R. Hall, PhD

Foreword by David Omotoso Stovall, PhD

African American Images
Chicago, Illinois

Dedicated to my brothers—
John "LJ" Hackney Jr. a.k.a. The Laid Back Lover
and
Larry J. Lennix a.k.a. SMASH
May you rest in power.

The harvest is past, the summer is ended, and we are not saved.

— JEREMIAH 8:20 (KING JAMES VERSION)

What, then, is the school of today, no matter whether public, private, or parochial? It is for the child what the prison is for the convict and the barracks for the soldier—a place where everything is being used to break the will of the child, and then to pound, knead, and shape it into a being utterly foreign to itself. I do not mean to say that this process is carried on consciously; it is but a part of a system which can maintain itself only through absolute discipline and uniformity; therein, I think, lies the greatest crime of present-day society.

—EMMA GOLDMAN

Life is to be lived, not controlled; and humanity is won by continuing to play in the face of certain defeat.

—RALPH ELLISON

If you ask for good schools, you aren't likely to get them. If you ask for jobs or economic investment, you won't get that either. But what we have learned, is that the one thing that poor folks of color can ask for and get are Police & Prisons.

—MICHELLE ALEXANDER

You have to act as if it were possible to radically transform the world. And you have to do it all the time.

—ANGELA Y. DAVIS

CONTENTS

Foreword by Dr. David Omotoso Stovall   *ix*

Preface   *xv*

Acknowledgments   *xxiii*

Intro   1

2007   17

    Aaliyah Camacho   18

    Audrey Bell   21

    Chris Wozniak   26

    Marcus Bridges   29

    Miguel Alvarez   33

    Quincy Washington   39

    Susan Kline   42

Year 2007: Questions, Reflections & Resources   55

2008   67

    Charmaine Johnson   68

Haley Robinson 84

Jocelyn Rawls 88

Patricia Wright 95

Rachel Booker 106

Ronald Hathaway 115

Tameika Eldridge 126

Year 2008: Questions, Reflections & Resources 133

2009 145

Chris Harris 146

Eduardo Hernandez 154

Isabelle Esperanza 166

Joseph Martinez 174

Lawrence Kittle 177

Lissette Lopez 188

Mary Taylor 191

Year 2009: Questions, Reflections & Resources 201

2011 211

Daniel Watson 212

Helen McConnell 220

Jeremy King 225

Year 2011: Questions, Reflections & Resources 237

Outro 245

FOREWORD

Containing the Results of Historical Theft

Scholar-activist Dr. kihana miraya ross poses a question in her public lectures and writings that is pertinent to this book: *What does it mean to exist as the result of a theft?* For some, the question may at first appear puzzling, but for many Black people the question makes perfect sense. Africans were kidnapped and brought to the shores of the Caribbean and the Western Hemisphere to work as unpaid labor for the White ruling class of Western Europe and their immediate descendants. In the process, Black people were dehumanized, made less-than, and isolated to the margins of society.

The myths of our criminality, insatiable sexuality, and perpetual inferiority have spanned centuries and show up in every aspect of life and understanding in the United States. Blackness has been made burdensome—it represents the dregs of society and everything that is wrong with it. More powerful is the ability of the ruling class to get

Black folks to internalize these beliefs and enact violence on each other in the name of White supremacy. Historically the rationale has been to contain the threat "for our own good." Fortunately, for some, we have always known this and have been willing to expose that lie for what it is—a ploy to rationalize gratuitous punishment on Black people for merely existing.

The goal of White supremacy has always been to maim, contain, isolate and eventually kill Black bodies because they best serve power if they are confined to spaces where their labor is controlled, education is limited, and wellness is next to nonexistent. For those of us who are a result of this theft, there is a clear connection between history and the truth of the present moment.

Dr. Horace Hall has taken it upon himself to tell a story that is both known and rejected by many. While many of us live amongst the realities of a police state, we are clear in our understanding of what it's like to feel that our lives are perpetually on lockdown. Given the fact that this is known by many, it is still rejected by the mainstream in their realization that the positioning of Black, Brown and Indigenous bodies as criminal before human is the proverbial foundation for life in the U.S.

The recently publicized police deaths of George Floyd, Breonna Taylor, Ahmaud Arbery and Tony McDade, while shocking to the White masses, serve as a brutal reminder that at any given moment we are reminded of our perpetual precariousness. Coupled with the global health pandemic of COVID-19, our deepening confinements allow us to sit in the certainty of what it means to exist under the pandemics of a potentially lethal pathogen, White supremacy and capitalism. As these realities are laid bare, *Always on Lockdown* is timely in that it pulls no punches in revealing a composite of stories that acknowledge the depth of the situation and the necessity for resistance.

As a lifelong Chicagoan, I can attest to Dr. Hall's assessment of our city as a place that feels like it is built to castigate anyone who is not White and wealthy. From parking meters with exorbitant fees to privatized toll roads, and from hyper-police presence/surveillance to gentrified neighborhoods once populated with working-class Peoples of Color, you can feel as if the city should have a billboard that reads: THANK YOU FOR ALLOWING US TO PUNISH YOU FOR LIVING HERE. This book informs us that schools are no different.

Dr. Hall and I agree that the language of the school-to-prison pipeline no longer captures the severity of the above condition. Depending on your social and geographic location in Chicago, school metal detectors, uniforms, silent lunches, locked bathrooms with no soap or toilet paper are not reflective of your school being "prison-like." If you are in a school in Chicago (or anyplace else in the world) that operates under these rules and logics, you are no longer in a space that values your humanity. Instead, you have been regulated to a carceral mechanism rooted in containment versus a relevant, positive environment centered in learning and inquiry. We are no longer describing a situation where the school provides a mechanism for you to reach prison. Instead, it is a circumstance where the school and the prison have become one.

For all intents and purposes, many young people in our city know very well that *the school and prison is the same thing.* This school/prison nexus reminds young people in Chicago that the place they are required to be for the vast majority of the day prioritizes containment over learning. In many of these same spaces, they are also over-tested and often lack essential resources like libraries and computer technologies. If it is difficult for you to fathom that this is happening in a 21st-century global city, then you do not know Chicago. Living here lets you know early on as to whose lives are considered valuable and who is deemed disposable.

At the same time, young people continue to refuse to accept what the world says about them. They know that they have been dehumanized. They are clear that many adults still expect them to sit in their suffering, while the world moves to drive knees into their necks (George Floyd) and to kill them while they are asleep (Breonna Taylor). They have demonstrated on the streets in multitudes, leading the largest mass movement in the history of the United States.

Young people have also pushed us to ponder abolition, Black feminist fugitivity and solidarity economies. Because their efforts are still in their early stages, it has yet to be seen where this moment takes us. In the interim, however, it has alerted the world to the connective tissues of health pandemics, White supremacy and capitalism. I remain deeply encouraged by young folks' efforts and work in tandem with them to change their conditions. Because it is a job that is for the long haul, I am confident in their capacity to make it happen.

As Dr. Hall has charged me with the task of providing a foreword for *Always on Lockdown*, I hope the contents of his book move you to think about what we are in and what we must do. Reform is unacceptable. The creation of something new is the only way out of this. Settling for more of the same is what got us here in the first place.

David Omotoso Stovall, PhD
Chicago, Illinois
August 4, 2020

PREFACE

The cops in my school
Be the ones on my block.
Stopped and frisked daily from my hoodie to my socks.
Now I'm late for class
But they don't give a shit.
Seeing my black ass
Like seeing guns and shit.
Wild cause they the ones packing.
Hallway terminators
Straight prison tracking.
Waiting for your ass just to fuck up.
Now you in a cell
You don't know what's up
With the charge they gave to you
Locked out of class plus homeroom too.
How we going to learn inside a human zoo?[1]

—QUINCY WASHINGTON,[2] AGE 17

The idea for this book was first sparked by Quincy, a high school student proclaiming himself as "The Lyrical Grand Empirical." He, along with 19 of his peers, took part in a nonprofit, school-based youth program that I started in 2000. It was designed to supplement socio-emotional learning in Chicago Public Schools (CPS) with a focus on teens interested in examining community spaces and expressing their issues through various curriculum formats: the arts, social media, public awareness campaigns, petitions, or community service.

During the early years of the program, I had one adult female and two adult males collaborating as core facilitators, who were also friends of mine. Each had formerly worked a number of years in CPS as an educator, counselor or mentor. I myself had taught for a number of years before leaving the system as well. Since the program's launch, we have been hosted in dozens of schools across the district.

Between February and May of 2006, we were contracted by Zapata High School[3] located in a working-class west side community. Its student body was 98% Black and Latinx—the typical composition of schools housing the program[4]. In its previous year, Zapata enrolled a number of transfer students from adjacent neighborhoods who either had their schools slowly phased out or immediately shut down due to the district's newly enacted policy, Renaissance 2010 (Ren 2010).

The compulsory integration of new enrollees into Zapata, according to school staff, yielded an uptick in racial and cultural discord amongst those students already attending. To help quell tensions, CPS distended its use of security personnel, as well as launching a series of youth development initiatives.

Zapata's principal scheduled our program meetings to be held twice a week, after school, for 90 minutes. Freshmen through seniors volunteered to take part. After a few "icebreaker" sessions, we invited our new members to pen and perform an original, self-authored piece about any topic relevant to their lives. This was one of many activities that we used to encourage young folk to voice their cultural identities and realities. From my program experiences, students, more often than not, were attracted to the art forms of poetry and rap as mediums for channeling what was most immediate to their lives. Zapata students proved no different. Conceived out of the proposed assignment was the Lyrical Grand Empirical's rhyme.

After Quincy delivered his verse, a spirited dialogue amongst program members ignited. Each candidly shared their own accounts of living and feeling criminalized by teachers, staff and security guards either at Zapata or other schools. According to them, if they jokingly pushed another student in the hallway, it was considered "assault and battery"; if they spoke too loudly in class, it was deemed "disturbing the peace." For virtually any misconduct, they attested to being unfairly placed in detention, suspended or taken into police custody. They then began drawing parallels between schools and prisons. I jotted down their responses on the whiteboard as quickly as I could:

Prisons	School
Controlling guards and warden	Controlling teachers and principal
Search and seizure by police	Search and seizure by police
Surveillance cameras	Surveillance cameras
(even in bathrooms)	(even in bathrooms)
Surveillance webcams	Surveillance webcams
Institutional uniforms	Institutional uniforms
No food from the outside	No food from the outside
"The Hole" (detention)	"The Hole" (detention)
Use of handcuffs	Use of handcuffs
Police presence in-/outside	Police presence in-/outside
Metal detectors	Metal detectors
CCTVs	CCTVs
Electromagnetic door locks	Electromagnetic door locks
Privatized food provider	Privatized food provided
Prisoners feeling powerless	Students feeling powerless
No rights and nobody cares	No rights and nobody cares

My colleagues and I had been in a number of Chicago schools where youth expressed legitimate complaints about their learning environments—from leaky roofs, congested classrooms and crappy cafeteria food to outdated textbooks, over-testing and culturally irrelevant curriculum. Zapata students now added one more item to the list: *jailed schooling.*

I recall feeling a sort of ambivalence during that program session. On the one hand, it was extremely rewarding to watch these young folk cogently demonstrate a level of critical consciousness about their world that would certainly make any parent or teacher proud; on the other hand, their testimonies plainly spoke to the heavy burdens of systemic racism that they had experienced in and outside of schools.

I carried similar weight growing up in hypersegregated Chicago as an adolescent Black male constantly navigating the serrated terrain of racially biased policing, intolerant teachers, and fears of rushed adult judgments and bodily regulation. The key difference between then and now was that CPS schools, comprising a majority of Black and Latinx students, were progressively executing zero tolerance policies, increasing police and security guard presence, utilizing omnipresent surveillance technologies, and handing down gross suspensions and expulsions that pushed many students farther away from their dreams and goals of achieving educational opportunities.

Taking Zapata members' prison-school comparisons beyond the classroom, facilitators and students jointly agreed to produce a public awareness document. On every page, we outlined to staff, faculty and administration the concerns of these young folks—from the criminalization of ordinary teenage behavior and vague and discriminatory school policies to the extreme uses of physical force against students in a place where they generally wanted to feel free and sheltered from authoritarian control over *their* bodies and minds. The finished document was placed into individual employee mailboxes.

March turned into April with no responses from the school— absolutely zero. I asked Zapata's principal if she had even received the document. She informed me that she had and her staff was still looking it over. Throughout the remaining weeks of the program, facilitators continued to engage members in discussions on school and community issues—police and gun violence, hypersegregation, and neighborhood disinvestment. Students even produced a video narrating their concerns, which they later uploaded onto YouTube. All the while, deafening silence from their school leaders.

The program ended in May with a culminating event of food, beverages and music. Every participant was honored for sharing their time, energy and honesty. Despite this festal end, weeks later I couldn't shake a nagging contradiction: How could Zapata's administration expect, even mandate through school compliance, that students be kind and deferential towards others while simultaneously immersing them into an uncompromising system of punishment and derision? And yet, if these youth were only channeling a single perspective, then why did not staff and faculty express, at the very least, some level of doubt or disagreement to our public awareness document?

The personal stories of Zapata students deeply resonated with me. I wondered how many other young people in CPS socially constructed the disciplinary design of their schools and how might their teachers, staff, parents and guardians perceive this phenomenon? These questions, along with my time at Zapata, serve as the underpinnings for the assemblage of this book. The following pages are thus an attempt to answer the above query, drawing on a collection of real and lived narratives from CPS participants between 2007 and 2011—a stretch of time marked by heavy school policing and discipline within classrooms and corridors of an education system largely occupied by low-income Students of Color.

PREFACE NOTES

[1] Collected March 2006.

[2] A pseudonym. The names of all individuals and schools agreeing to participate in this research have been changed for the purpose of anonymity and confidentiality so that any data participants have provided cannot be traced back to them in reports, presentations and other forms of dissemination. The names of CPS schools nonaffiliated with research contributors remain intact.

[3] A pseudonym.

[4] Data retrieved from Chicago Public Schools website: https://www.cps.edu/about/district-data/

ACKNOWLEDGMENTS

My deepest thanks go to all of the interview participants
appearing in this book.
I truly appreciate you sharing your time, energy and
personal stories.
Peace & Solidarity,
HRH

INTRO

Always on Lockdown:
An Oral History of Policing and Discipline Inside Public Schools

Renaissance 2010, Gentrification and School Closures: The Chicago Context

This book is about security measures used in Chicago public schools. It is about young bodies moving, without visible shackles, throughout learning environments suffused with surveillance, discipline and punishment. The following text offers real-life accounts by school participants disclosing how their schooling institutions are not ostensibly passive symbols or containers, but rather spaces where exerted carceral power transfixes human lives within a matrix of penalizing rules and political authority.

Schools, as hierarchical structures, implicitly and explicitly reveal the ways in which students conform, resist and establish physical and social presence within the austere disciplinary conditions surrounding them. In our age of growing surveillance and police presence, *Always on Lockdown: An Oral History of Policing and Discipline Inside Public Schools* communicates relationalities between Peoples of Color and boundaries, control and compliance, privilege and neglect, subjection and opposition, and struggle for institutional change.

This book begins in 2006, two years after Chicago Mayor Richard M. Daley announced, with much hype, his proposal to create 100 new public schools.[1] Dubbed "Renaissance 2010" (Ren 2010), it was his pledge to improve education by supporting high-performing schools, while closing those deemed as "failing" and depleting the city's already anemic budget. Public funds for the policy trickled in slowly, but private capital tallying $70 million secured its advancement.

Daley's initiative, however, was met with immediate rebuke from the Chicago Teachers Union (CTU), community groups and parents distressed by the number of schools slated for shutdown—60 in total. Their main concern centered on the social and psychological blow closings would have on Black and Latinx communities, forcing thousands of children to move from school to school. This policy would also uphold the city's long-established two-tiered school system—the first, a narrow tier of high quality schools readily accessible for well-advantaged families; the second, a much broader tier yet with fewer resources for the mostly low-income, minority students attending.

To understand the multiple impacts of Ren 2010 on Chicago Public School (CPS) participants, one must first be familiar with Chicago's political and economic landscape. The city's enduring legacy of racial segregation can be traced back to the mid-1800s through redlining, blockbusting, restrictive covenants and other systemic racist practices. In every direction throughout its metropolitan area, lines of demarcation were drawn across neighborhoods, blocks and even street corners, riving groups by race and class. These borders of inequality helped establish Chicago's reputation as a "dual city"—one north with vibrant businesses, soaring property values, and mostly white-collar citizens of formal educational background; the second, quarantined south, east, west and away from the business district, largely Black, Latinx, undereducated, and living middle, low, to no income.

In recent decades, local politicians have exacerbated Chicago's segregation via exclusionary zoning practices, making outcomes for struggling minorities worse. This has been observed in cases of gentrification, where public and private capital investments have commodified and transformed the geography of economically crippled areas into middle- and upper-class "premium ZIP codes." Longtime inhabitants, delegitimized by wealthier residents and unable to afford urban renewal, often relocate to urban or suburban enclaves of similar race and class background.

Displaced residents, upon reaching their new surroundings, are often unwanted by existing community members who consider uprooted arrivals a threat to already scarce resources such as employment opportunities, living quarters and schooling options. While rising housing costs, unbroken segregation, and persistent community disinvestment are forms of symbolic violence, the visible by-product of each has manifested in intercultural physical hostility within mostly urban Black and Brown neighborhoods.

Chicago's public school system is a microcosm of its broader economic and racial ghettoization. Ren 2010 coincided well with renewal projects trending across the city as both the public and private sector desired greater management over municipal capital. Between 2001 and 2009, CPS closed 73 schools due to low academic performance. Ninety percent just so happened to be in majority working-class and low-income Black communities, and to a lesser degree, Latinx ones.

During this same period, the district launched 87 new schools, with 62 being charters. Less than a quarter of these schools, however, were achieving at or above the state's average on the Illinois Standards Achievement Test (ISAT). In 2013, with the city still financially sluggish, Rahm Emanuel, during his second year as the city's new mayor, shut down 50 public schools—95% of which were serving Black and Latinx youth. Despite heated resident backlash against the closings, as well as zero data to suggest that "choice" schools were more viable than traditional ones, CPS continued to approve applications for new charter and contract schools.

With the bulk of school closures befalling Black and Brown communities, particularly in 2013, disproportionate numbers of families, whether old or new to their neighborhood, were forced to find other educational options that unfortunately involved their children having to cross unsafe gang territories in order to reach a free and appropriate public education. Chicago families were well aware of the dangers of youth traveling too far beyond their block to get to school and back home safely.

At the start of Ren 2010, the average number of CPS students fatally shot in their communities was between 10 and 15. That number rose to 27 between 2006 and 2008. By the end of 2008, nearly 80% of city homicides occurred in 22 Black and Latinx communities—the very same areas where school closures took place. Before 2009 ended, there were a total of 34 CPS student deaths by way of physical or gun violence. One example made national news with a cell phone recorded video of Fenger High School[2] student Derrion Albert being beaten to death by several boys who transferred into Fenger after having their neighborhood school shut down.

To reduce violent student skirmishes, CPS initially leaned heavily on its zero tolerance policy. Employed by thousands of schools across the country, this harsh disciplinary measure is used to deal with student behavioral problems. For example, two leading student infractions are acts of defiance and physical altercations, which can result in suspension (lasting five or more days), expulsion or transfer to a specialized school.[3]

Boys, in general, are much more likely to be expelled than girls. Nationwide, Black males are by far expelled more than any other cultural group. An illustration of this disparity comes from CPS's own 2008–09 reported data. At the time, Black males comprised 23% of the student population, yet accounted for 61% of those expelled. Latin males were 20% of the population, but made up 15% of all expulsions. These two groups were in stark contrast to White males, who in that same year comprised 4% of CPS's population, yet constituted only 1% of district-wide expulsions.[4]

After much pressure from families and community activists disturbed by high expulsion levels, CPS officially scrapped its zero tolerance policy in 2009, substituting it for restorative justice practices. Despite overall expulsion rates dipping over the next six years, the number of high school in-school suspensions actually doubled for Black students, while remaining the same for youth of other ethnicities. What is more, the district maintained a steady partnership with the Chicago Police Department (CPD) and the Fraternal Order of Police (FOP).

For CPS and city officials, wanton student aggression justified heavier patrolling of schools and neighborhoods. Support for this first arrived in 2007 from the Illinois State Board of Education (ISBE) in a $4 million package. Over the next three years, $32 million of ISBE funding was spent on 96 CPS schools for blue light cameras on nearby blocks, along with in-school X-ray scanning machines, closed-circuit TV (CCTV) monitors, de-escalation conflict training for staff and faculty, and of course, full-time police officers and SROs.[5]

Caged Classrooms—More Than a Metaphor

What was puzzling to me about the city expanding its policing during this time was that growing up in Chicago my peers and I didn't perceive law enforcement as a body to protect us. In truth, they simply weren't meant to be trusted, especially when friends, parents, aunts, uncles and cousins explicitly warned us about police misconduct. Everything "five-o"[6] signified—from their badges and guns to paddy wagons and police stations—was rife with a long, racist history of brutality against Black folks. This went for the same inside schools.

Any interaction with cops would surely lead me and my peers to being "spread-eagled," harassed, and even mortally wounded by our refusal to be singled out or taken away. Yet, public consensus to have classrooms and corridors patrolled by police and SROs, especially in the wake of nationwide school shootings, reinforced a "new normal." Schools, now more than ever before, began resembling structural clones of airports, military bases and prisons, where students could be falsely construed as enemy combatants of the State.

We often hear young people complain that their school is like a jail—a direct contrast to the non-institutional freedoms they cherish on playgrounds, in video games, online chatrooms and all else non-school. Their impression, however, may not be too far-off as the roots of both institutions reveal a deeply organic relationship that begins with kindred structural architecture and scale. One need only visit a modern-day urban schoolhouse to observe brutal brick and plexiglass windows enclosed by barbed wire and chain-link fences.

Upon entry, caged aesthetics are accentuated by long, double-loaded corridors with electromagnetic door locks, hallway video surveillance cameras, metal detectors, X-ray screening machines and officers displaying bulletproof vests, scanning wands and, of course, pistols. Often reserved for inner-city youth, almost every American public school—urban, suburban or rural—adopts these measures in some fashion, ranging from the strikingly bold and intimidating to the slyly camouflaged and unnoticed.

Broader comparisons between schools and other corrective institutions reveal the ways in which policies and practices are used to oppress cultural groups and internalize differences.[7] Just as the criminal justice system, for example, dualistically functions to protect the most privileged while persecuting the most disadvantaged, schools replicate the same racial and class divide.

We see this in highly-resourced, majority-White academies that abundantly expose their students to critical thinking curriculum and minimal police supervision versus divested "apartheid schools"[8] that routinely "drill and kill" pupils through rote memorization and standardized testing. Educational research has noted that youth attending the latter, and who are learning disabled, impoverished or homeless, experience a greater frequency of regulation, suspension and expulsion compared to their well-heeled counterparts.[9]

Like the hypersegregated urban crucible, apartheid schools have relied heavily on neoteric, "tough on crime" policies that are more intent on over-policing and disciplining learners than giving them high-caliber academic and social support. For Black and Brown youth living through normalized bodily and subjective regulation, the school complex is more than a metaphor for jail—*it is jail*. These "instructional warehouses" force students—consciously and unconsciously—to conform to micro- and macro-systems of racial and class difference, of internment and isolation. This is a daily curriculum witnessed and learned, and it indeed shares parallels with other securitized institutions.

Undeniably, schools that fail to adequately educate students of color, dismissing them as "at-risk," "uneducable," and "oppositional" and then punish them for it, are far from being affirming and liberatory spaces. They are instead pipelines of criminalization, prelusive cages to incarceration where a "one-size-fits-all" curriculum and an "all-seeing eye" limit them from openly challenging the status quo and transforming institutions and themselves for a better life as they define it.

Always on Lockdown: An Oral History of Policing and Discipline Inside Public Schools

The following pages are a gathering of human experiences tangled up in a larger web of institutional rules and norms. The compilation of personal stories/interviews collected, from 2007 to 2011, are essentially the ways in which contributors—students, parents, teachers, administrators and police officers—socially constructed technologies of control and discipline within a schooling system that is disproportionately low-income Black and Latinx youth.

No doubt, there is nothing new beneath the sun. Yet, the narratives and counter-narratives lining the pages of this book are more than simply a chronicle of the past. Instead, they are, in my view, vital offerings that provide intimate glimpses into a moment in time, enlightening us to then and now and even future issues of racial inequality and the (de-) humanization of People of Color. Indeed, history is not a dead thing. Historical context is indispensable because it is how we remember and acknowledge our past that informs today's struggles against social injustices.

My personal conviction in bringing these accounts to the fore of sociopolitical discourse was often interrupted by the daily challenges of family, university teaching, other writing projects and my youth activist work. Nevertheless, the force driving me to finally complete this endeavor was repeatedly seeing up close and personal, as well as through daily news reports, the physical and psychic scars being endured by Black and Latinx peoples—displacement, school violence, neighborhood shootings, and police abuses.

What is more, virtually absent from blanket media coverage were detailed accounts of those acutely affected by large-scale school and community disinvestment of Black and Brown futures. Thus, it became increasingly clear to me that the stories I had collected needed to see the light of day and that there was no better medium for expanding our senses about the impacts of "Ren 2010 life" in Chicago than by bringing this book to readers.

Without question, we each possess a lens by which the world is perceived and grasped. In trying to comprehend what was happening in Chicago communities during Ren 2010, I was deeply concerned with how folk created, negotiated, reinforced and revised meaning within a specific context of human action. Drawing on cultural anthropological methods, I put myself in the position of an "information gatherer."

From my research approach, I became acquainted with the ways in which the participants I had access to—all of whom were knowledgeable, articulate, thoughtful, well-meaning and forthright— viewed discipline policies and how their perspectives might differ or correspond with my own. Interestingly enough, the longer I sat with this book's contributors and gained their trust as a relative outsider, the more openly they shared their perspectives about a pivotal time in Chicago school reform and its impact on school and community spaces.

The social scientist within me initially wanted to take these narratives and filter them through some sort of theoretical lens. Yet, I withdrew believing that this would unduly limit the scope of the lives being presented here while passing on to you, the reader, my subjective interpretations of their existence.

As opposed to obscuring this collection of day-to-day, on the ground realities with scientific theories or analyses, I instead offer my own thoughts, questions and resources for readers to consider, reflect on, and perhaps even act upon. These can be found at the end of each yearly section. Admittedly, however, if there was any framework that guided my thinking during this research project, it was: *Mass schooling is and has continuously been about regulating young minds and bodies. School policing is just another device to secure control over people's lives.*

Despite my lens, this book is not a reproach of surveillance technologies; nor is it a manual for improving policing strategies in order to somehow make schools feel safer or less "criminal." Rather, this work concerns itself with real and symbolic institutional lessons brought on by Ren 2010. This is an anthology of Chicago school staff, teachers, students and parents speaking openly about their relationships and struggles with these lessons and what others can learn from this "instruction."

In no way are the interviews presented here intended to generalize the entire U.S. educational system. They might, however, provide some mirrored image as to what other school participants nationwide, whether urban, suburban or rural, experience in the wake of disciplinary policies and procedures, of privilege and neglect, of obedience and resistance, and of hope and change for anyone surviving castigatory learning environments.

In its origin and evolution, *Always on Lockdown* is a "voice" project. My use of voice in this framework is devoted to uncovering oppressive societal acts and the ways in which people give meaning and construct reality in the presence of such phenomena. Thus, it was essential for me to move beyond surface conversations and into a critical dialogue with participants about how they comprehend, question and live through securitized public terrains. While I felt that some were hesitant to censure their school/workplace (and rightly so), others candidly disclosed their opposition to institutional controls, as well as their desire for this aspect of schooling to be less callous and more humane.

There is a plethora of books detailing the impact that security measures have on disciplining America's youth—from Devine's *Maximum Security* (1996) and Casella's *At Zero Tolerance* (2001) to Kupchik's *Homeroom Security* (2010), Fuentes's *Lockdown High* (2011) and Rios's *Human Targets* (2017), just to name a few. Building on this literature, I felt it was also essential to know and to preserve the voices of Chicago residents who are rarely heard, validated or even involved in policy making decisions. Borrowing from Studs Terkel's literary style— e.g., *Working* (1974) and *Race* (1992)—every page of this volume is predominantly lined with the stories of contributors. Their driving narratives not only function as an archive for future historians to draw upon, but also a "counter-curriculum" of untold or forgotten schooling experiences that we can all undoubtedly learn from.

Always on Lockdown: An Oral History of Policing and Discipline Inside Public Schools is not meant to be strictly ivory tower text. Rather, this volume seeks to genuinely inform and arouse as many audiences as possible to experienced institutional control that is sadly not much different today than when these interviews were first conducted. Students of history, education, sociology, criminology and ethnic studies will find meaning in this work as it elucidates the historicity of racial and class oppression in Chicago, the nation and abroad.

For activists and organizers, this book affirms that, once again, history is not a dead thing and by recalling it, we might enhance the ways in which we organize and challenge present-day class and racial injustices. Alternatively, for those seeing themselves as distant from this phenomenon, I hope that you will still engage this book, as it seeks to reveal how normalized relations of power not only dominate the lives of Peoples of Color, but *all* human beings within our shared social thread.

INTRO NOTES

[1]When Renaissance 2010 the was first introduced, Chicago Public School (CPS) administrators called for the closure of up to 60 low-performing neighborhood schools and the opening of 100 new "choice" or "Renaissance" schools—a blend of one-third neighborhood and high-performance public schools and two-thirds privatized charter/contract schools. Charters are public schools that are independently run, while receiving tax dollars from the public sphere, as well as donations from the private sector. According to Chicago Public Schools' website, "contract schools are public schools open to all CPS students. These schools are operated by private entities under contract with CPS to provide an additional education option for students." There are no attendance boundaries and students across the city can apply.

[2] Fenger Academy is a four–year CPS high school. It is located in the Roseland community on the far south side of Chicago. The school is approximately 95% Black, 2% Latinx and 1% other. Ninety-one percent of its student body is considered low-income. Both its enrollment and graduation rate is at 100% with an average SAT score of 831.

[3] See: Han, S. (2017). *Corporal punishment in rural schools: Student problem behaviours, academic outcomes and school safety efforts.* New York, NY: Springer Publishing Co.

[4] See: Consortium on Chicago School Research (May 2015). *Discipline practices in Chicago schools: Trends in the use of suspensions and arrests (Executive Summary)*. Chicago, IL: University of Chicago Press.

[5] A school resource officer (SRO) is defined by the federal government as a "sworn law enforcement officer responsible for safety and crime prevention in schools." SROs can be deployed by a public police department or private police agency for a community-oriented policing assignment in collaboration with one or more schools. As of 2018, the State of Illinois mandated that SROs receive special training for dealing with adolescents in areas of de-escalation, crisis intervention and cyberbullying.

[6] Slang term for law enforcement.

[7] See: Foucault, M. (1978). *The history of sexuality*. (OKS Print.) New York, NY: Pantheon Books.

[8] "Apartheid schools" is a term used to describe high poverty, high-minority schools that are less than 1% White, where students frequently have lower grades, lower graduation rates, and a lifetime of lower achievement versus other students in more diverse districts.

[9] See: Losen, D. J. (Ed.). (2015). *Closing the school discipline gap: Equitable remedies for excessive exclusion*. New York, NY: Teachers College Press.

YEAR 2007

"It's definitely a health hazard."
AALIYAH CAMACHO[1]

For Chicagoans, "K-Town" is a familiar nickname that identifies an area on the city's west side. Officially, it stretches between North Lawndale and West Garfield Park. Yet, for those residents who have long, deep-seated historical roots, K-Town's borders "unofficially" extend further north through West Humboldt Park and south into the Little Village community. The avenues running north to south through these four neighborhoods begin with the letter K— Kilpatrick, Kenton, Kenneth, Kolmar, Kilbourn, Kostner, Kirkland, Kolin, Kildare, Keeler, Kedvale, Karlove, Keystone and Komensky.

Aaliyah Camacho is 16. Since third grade, she has moved several times with her family throughout K-Town. "We were always looking for cheaper rent, more space, less gangs." Despite her number of relocations, Aaliyah states that she's been able to maintain close relationships with childhood friends. In her first year at Zapata, she was not exactly an honor roll student. She had a hard time connecting with her academics and her teachers. She contemplated dropping out more than once, but didn't want to let her family down. "I'm a first-generation high school student. No one in my family has made it this far and I can see why."

So, I'll begin with our principal, well, our former principal. I made, you know, a few bad decisions and was about to be kicked out. I was like whatever. Last month, I had ditched class to go for a job interview and was thinking I'll just get a GED. I was waiting on my test scores and stuff. Fast forward to last week, I was on the same stuff, you know, ditching class, walking the hallways.

The principal heard my name on his walkie-talkie and said I was getting 10 days. I'm talking like 10 days just for not being in class? But, he didn't know that. He just heard my name and it was something about my mom was downstairs. When I saw her, she was like, 'You got 10 days.' I get to snapping on him and stuff like, 'You can't suspend me for no reason. You just heard my name. That's it.'

The principal told me that he can do anything he wants. That's how he gets down on me. He would suspend me for spitting outside *off* of school grounds if he wanted to. That's why I was like I'm not taking 10 days. But I did take three in-school days, you know, I had to barter with him a little bit.

As for security guards, well, we've had some who beat students with cuffs. We had one named Moe. I think that was his name. We called him 'Jock.' It was like two days ago in my sixth period lunch when my friend got in trouble over some weed. She had a $10 bag of weed. So, the guard we call 'Jock,' grabbed her, wrestled with her and took it from her, trying to get her locked up. So I had got mad and started cursing him out or whatever. He didn't care. He was just shady.

There'll be days in sixth period lunch where it's like a little wall in the back and there'll be like seven dudes over there shooting dice and Jock will tell them when the other security guards come that way to break it up. He'll let that happen. But when my girl got one bag of weed, you want to lock her up. That's crazy.

Another guard who petrifies me, we call him 'Mr. Clean' cause he has bald, shiny head. Man, can he eat a lunch. Anyway, we were walking down the hallway and Mr. Clean said something to one of the guys I was with. And, you know kids, you know how we are, they start talking crazy stuff to him.

So, instead of trying to calm them down, Mr. Clean grabbed one of them, threw him to the ground, put him in a choke hold until his face turned red. He started yelling at the other security guards saying my friend tried to swing on him. I'm right here watching the whole thing. I'm like he didn't even do that. He didn't deserve that. He was just going to class. It was too crazy. The rest of us just walked off.

I mean sometimes, you know, I'm not going to lie. When a fight do breaks out, the kids want to see it, so everybody runs and looks. Then, everybody's crowding and security guards can't clear everybody out, so they just spray Mace in the air and run out the crowd and let everybody go nuts, you know? It's not safe. Especially for me cause I got asthma. That's for real. It's definitely a health hazard.

You know, my friends call *their* school 'The P'—it stands for prison or prisoners or something like that. We should do that here. One time, our principal actually had a S.W.A.T. team to come through. It was after school, but there were students still in the building. I was here. It was crazy. I've never seen so many cop cars at one high school. They're walking through the hallways with AKs all because of a girl fight. It was the whole cheerleading team. I swear. They had Taser guns and all that.

I don't blame guards for having to do their jobs. Sometimes it's on us [students] too. I mean, you can go to class, you know? You don't have to watch the fights. You can go to class. You have a choice. Do what you have to do. It's your choice. If you want to look at the fight and after that go talk about it with everybody in the hallway knowing you should take your ass to class, well do what you have to do. But, there's times when a fight goes down and security instantly locks the floor gates. After that, you can't get to class, even if you wanted to. I've been trapped like that before. You can't even get past the fight.

So, you're trying to go around, but you get caught back there. Now, you have to try to keep out of sight cause the cameras are on you. Then, the principal looks at the video and that gets you and everybody else in the hallway suspended. Every face he sees, he looks up and suspends them. I remember getting 10 days just for getting stuck in the hallway. The principal looks at the cameras and writes your name down. Then, you get suspended. When you get back, the same thing happens again. So what's the point? It's a cycle, it's continuous. You know what I'm saying?

September 2007

"...those little black globes..."
AUBREY BELL[2]

Aubrey Bell is 17 years old and set to graduate from Jo Ann Robinson High School[3]—a selective enrollment school. She lives about a mile from Robinson on the city's south side in a majority Black neighborhood. She is studying business administration with a focus on entrepreneurship. Aubrey states that she wants to major in fashion design in college and later open her own clothing store. "The world isn't ready for what I'm going to bring. I have so many ideas to help empower women on how they look, dress and feel."

I've been wearing school uniforms my whole life. I've been at private schools most of my life. I've had to wear Catholic [school] uniforms. At first, I didn't like it but now, I like it because I know if we didn't have uniforms then, I probably wouldn't have anything to wear [giggles]. And then too, like with the uniforms, I guess anybody could just come into the school with the same uniform and you'd know they were a student. But, it's like harder for them to come in if they don't have one. If a student didn't wear their uniform, they'd have to wear a big, bright T-shirt that says, 'out of uniform' and then get a detention right after school.

I didn't like uniforms at first because it's more comfortable to be in your own clothes and we [students] couldn't show our own personal style. You know, like sometimes your clothes show your personality. At our school, we wear our uniforms. We might mix it up to show our own personal style, to be different, but there's a basic uniform we all have to wear.

Uniforms and school safety isn't really an issue, but like—well, at least at my school it's not an issue. You know, my school, we're kind of like the elite of the Chicago public schools because we're selective enrollment and they don't let just anybody go to our school. You have to be accepted into it, so it's like we don't get bad kids. We've probably had, over the last four years that I've actually been there, about three fights. I just think that if we didn't wear uniforms—honestly, the community around my school is not the safest at all. Uniforms help us know who's who inside the school gates.

We do have metal detectors, though. There are about 800 students at our school, but we only have one that's working. It's pretty annoying too because you can't be late for first period. Everyone has to go through it, but imagine when it's cold outside and lines are outside the doors. Students are late for class because of the detector and it takes forever to get through it. And, I know it's policy and it's necessary with all that's going on in the world. It's just sad that we have to have them but, you know, the world is going through some crazy things right now.

What's really crazy is that I don't feel much safer because of them. People, you know, hide things and there are ways to get things inside and they find ways to do that. Occasionally, security guards will search students.

You know, I don't think the detectors and searches bother them. We all know that it's a policy thing and what's going on in the world. We can never be too safe. We can't be naïve to what's going on or what could happen as far as like the threat at Lane Tech or wherever. I think it's just policy and it's just something that needs to happen— some people might feel a little uncomfortable about it but I think that those are the precautions that we need to take with everything that's going on.

We also have cameras in random places. They're in the hallways and staircases. I'd say mostly in places people don't even pay attention to— just all around the school. They're these little black things, like a small globe. They're not visible. Well, they're visible, if you look of course. But, they're not visible if you don't pay attention [pointing to a ceiling-mounted security camera in the room]. People don't pay attention to them, but they're there. I personally don't mind them as long they're not in like private places [giggles].

We have security guards to break up fights mostly. Well, they would like break it up. I think they know how to do that. We have one security guard at the front door in the morning. Then, we have like two or three uniformed police officers, but they don't roam the hallway. They just sit at the front door. I guess to patrol that area, the lobby part. Then, they'll be in the lunchroom sometimes, but they don't roam the hallways. I think they're pretty laid back.

We don't really do anything bad because there's not really anything wrong at our school. I don't feel threatened in the environment. There hasn't been any situation that made me feel, 'Oh well, I'm scared and I'm happy the police are here.' Of course, they're doing their job. But, as far as like around the premises of the school, I guess I'm happy that they're there. I just don't think they have to do that much inside the school. It's really what's outside the school gates.

I live at 79th and Damen and it's not a good neighborhood. We got those little black globes to catch crime on the street. It doesn't make me feel any safer though because I know when it flashes there's something wrong with my community. I can't be outside doing whatever I want. Like, I don't feel that my sister and brother are safe. They could walk to school, but they don't. They have to take the bus now.

So, when you're going down 79th Street, you meet a lot of crazy people and it doesn't make me feel good or safe. It's like I wonder if those police officers or people who watch the videos from the black globes understand this. And, I'm pretty sure they don't because everything that was going on before they set them up is still going on now.

Police officers lined up outside of certain schools. I think that's another big issue, the fact that—and I was actually talking to my friend about it—when they closed their schools because of Renaissance 20 something, there were gangs inside those schools. Those gangs are getting separated and dispersed into different schools in which there are other gangs, and they're mixing together.

That's when you see a big need for security because there is this whole rivalry. That's what starts a lot the violence in those schools and neighborhoods. When they change those schools like they do communities, they get fights and brawling. But, where are they going to put the students? They need a place to put them. It's just not right that it's done and some politicians don't think about the kids and the families. I just think the whole system needs a reconstruction period. I just don't want students to be products of their environment.

I think security is more about policy than it is protection. Maybe just after 9/11 people believed it was about protection. Now it's just about policy and we have to do it because it's been happening for a while. We keep doing it because that's what some think is keeping us safe. I'm not saying it's not, but maybe there's an alternative.

A student shouldn't be kicked out of the school. I know it depends on what a student brings in and, of course, there should be repercussions and consequences to what he's doing. I just think schools are so quick to get rid of students without understanding their problems—like, what's happening at home, are you being bullied, you know, what's going on with you?

Instead of hiring security, what about more teachers? How about hiring more social workers or even people who are activists or people who could help students get jobs? There are so many kids that fall through the cracks and people don't see it. They just brush them under the table.

Not every school has the same budget or resources. Schools with more money get better things. It's a class and political issue. There are over 600 schools in the CPS system and they're not all getting the same resources. That's why the students are doing what they're doing. I feel like Chicago is one, if not the most, segregated cities in the country. And, that segregation alone has a lot to do with our school system also being segregated.

Why aren't the funds divided evenly and why aren't hurting schools getting the resources that they need? It's because of the environments they're in. If you change that, I think that has a lot to do with the issues that these schools are facing. Like one problem is because of another problem, and that problem is because of another problem. It's one giant cycle of problems that nobody wants to tackle it because they want to continue putting Band-Aids over it without looking at real issues. That's all they're doing.

December 2007

"Trust is important."
CHRIS WOZNIAK[4]

Chris Wozniak is 15 and a sophomore at Howard Langley College Prep.[5] It is one of CPS' 11 selective enrollment schools that provide accelerated

academic programs to meet the needs of Chicago's most advanced students.
Chris is extremely passionate about environmental sciences and says, "My
school offers academically challenging classes that I know will prepare me
for my field when I go to college."

At my high school, we don't wear uniforms. But, at my Catholic
elementary school, we had to wear uniforms. I like school without
uniforms a lot better because it's more comfortable. You get to wear
what you want, see how people are, and see their style even if you don't
really know them. Otherwise, with uniforms, everyone is the same.

We have two metal detectors, but only one works in the morning.
So, there's like two lines coming into school and they'll just like pull
out random people to get searched. They'll pull you out, go through
your bag, and maybe pat you down. I really don't mind because I have
nothing to hide, so I don't care.

But, we're also a small school too and everyone knows each other,
so if someone does bring a gun to school or something like that the
teachers would find out about it. And, I think that's because there's
a lot of trust at our school. There was this whole incident that went
on at Lane Tech[6] and I guess Lane's security didn't take it seriously or
something like that. Whenever things happen at our school, someone
always comes forward and lets students know, the administration
know, and we take it seriously. So, there's a lot of trust there.

In our school, the cameras are built into the architecture. It's a new
school, so you can't really tell that they're cameras. It's like this little
thing sticking out of the wall and it looks like it's supposed to be there.
They're in hallways, but not in classrooms. I didn't find out about them

until halfway through freshman year. My friend brought a water gun to school and he was like spraying people in the halls and when he went down to the lunchroom, security called him out on it.

We have three security guards at my school, but like everybody knows them by name and they're like more of a friend I guess than an actual security guard. They usually watch the security screens, so they're there to do that. They don't do much else. They just like walk around and talk to students. They're in uniforms, but if anything were to happen, I don't think you could rely on them to protect you. We've never had a fight before, so I mean what would they do?

Security to me is people in charge of making sure you're supposed to be where you're supposed to be. At Langley, I guess everyone knows where they're supposed to be, so there's not really a need for a lot of crowd control. Maybe it depends on the student body. You're not really a threat. They just want to make sure you're where you're supposed to be.

If there are any alternatives to metal detectors and police, I think you just have to replace them with trusting students. If you don't have that much security, then I guess people have to learn to trust each other. I mean, some people want to see if they can get stuff past the detectors, but, that's a small group. Trust is important. At my school, we trust each other. Students trust teachers and I think teachers trust us to do the right thing. So, all the security other schools use, we don't need it or want it.

Another thing is having resources to help students emotionally. At my school, we have a wellness center that is like separate from the counseling office. So, we have a social worker, I guess, coming from

Swedish Covenant Hospital.[7] You can go talk to them during your lunch period or before or after school. That's another alternative to police.

December 2007

"Police not here to uplift."
MARCUS BRIDGES[8]

Marcus Bridges is a 16-year-old sophomore attending Horizons Charter School[9] on the south side. He is new to his school and neighborhood. Marcus, his mom and 12-year-old brother moved from the west side to the Bronzeville[10] neighborhood. "We like where [we] stay now. There's less empty homes and businesses, plus Mom is closer to work." He enjoys graphic design and plans to attend California Institute for the Arts upon graduation.

We wear uniforms at my high school. I didn't like school uniforms at first, but I like them now because the whole thing people do is just put a uniform on and then they can wear it for a week. It was the color I didn't like at first. When I first started wearing them, it was in middle school and our shirts were purple and white, but they changed it. Our pants were tan. Now, in high school, it's a black shirt with beige pants.

As for metal detectors, my school doesn't have them. I think because it's in a safe community and like mostly the security guards and the teachers pretty much know each other, so we really don't need it. We all know each other. We all friends. If you did bring anything like a gun or weapon to the school, it's a strong consequence at the end, so nobody would be bringing any. And if somebody would even think of bringing a knife or a gun to school, we would be like, 'Oh no, don't do that. If you have a problem, you don't have to use no weapon because if you have a weapon you're going to jail.' Like I said, it's a strong consequence.

We have about six security guards, but really three because they switch shifts. They're at the main door and patrol who comes in. The only time we need security is just for them to walk through the hallway to make sure that everybody is in their classroom and that nobody is running around the halls and stuff like that. If they do anything for like a fight, they'll just tell that student to sit down, and the student sits down.

If they want to jump back and start fighting, they know they'll get five to 10 days suspension. On average, we have about two fights a month. It's just small stuff. It's not really fighting or brawls. It's more like arguing. Boys might be play wrestling, but if there's a big, big fight, it's the girls testing each other—either way and you getting 10 days.

Inside the school, I don't think guards are protecting us. I think it's really just to watch us—to be like invasive, to make sure you is in your place, to make sure you is in your classroom, doing what you gotta do, not wandering the hallways, to make sure you don't tag or mess with anything.

Some schools have heavy security and some don't because it's not safe for students outside the building. There are people outside want to fight us. It's not too long ago that my school had gangs going to it. The principal kicked them out and now the gangs think we're trying to run the school. So, they come out at the end of the day and try to test us and we get into fights.

I live at 43rd and Indiana. There ain't nothing over there but stupid crackheads. Crackheads and drug addicts and that's all you see, up and down the street. They be like, 'Hey man, you know where I can get a little something-something?' You just keep on walking and you keep on seeing them.

It's supposed be safe over there now because there's no more projects and they're building new condos. They even built a new police station on 35th and Indiana. They said that would be good too because now when we call 9-1-1 and we won't be put on hold. But, we still being put on hold. The question I have is who are the new condos and police station for? It ain't for the crackheads. It ain't for the gangs. I think there's a change coming.

The change I've been seeing is actually kind of pathetic. Basically, if there are five gangs in one school and that school closes down, you've got to put them into other schools. And, instead of giving those schools good teachers and administration, they think putting police officers there is really going to make a difference. I talk to people who go to these schools and they say it's like walking into jail, being searched and locked away. I've heard police have come into classes and put students in handcuffs. Why treat me like a criminal, if I'm not a criminal? That's the whole point. They're treating them like criminals.

So now everybody who's in that system, who goes through it, now they're used to that and they're becoming a product of that environment. It's like a lot of kids think they have nothing to lose because they're in a system that's set up against them. It feels like you're already in prison. You're always on lockdown. I'm already being forced to do stuff, told to sit here, shut up and do this. It really doesn't matter to them. So, it's like okay if I bring a gun to school, who cares?

The real change needs to happen without security. That mean, more counselors, less police. The only counselor at my school is for the LD [learning disabled] kids. That's it. The only other time we get counselors or like social workers is for the other kids that have problems with anger management or they go crazy a little bit. That's the only kid that gets the opportunity to talk to them. So, kids don't get reached before they get too crazy.

When we have stuff in our head or on our chest that we want to put out, the people that we end up talking to is the principal or the assistant principal. And, you know the principal is going to call the police or they going to call their lawyers and say, 'This person is a little crazy. He might go and do something crazy' or they call the parents. Now, why you going to contact our parents, when sometimes the stuff we got on our chest, our parents can't help us with? You know, we need outlets.

I also think we need to have people uplifting students and teaching them different things about respecting and feeling good about themselves, showing them better things. Then, they won't think about the negative stuff like gangs or drugs, if they have people supporting them like that. Police not here to uplift. We need uplifting and it's needed now.

December 2007

"...I go through the grapevine."
MIGUEL ALVAREZ[11]

Chicago Lawn, commonly referred to as Marquette Park, stretches from 6700 South to 71st Street and from California Avenue to Central Park Avenue. It encompasses 77 neighborhoods, along with the largest park on that side of Chicago—Marquette Park. For most of the 20th century, inhabitants of the area were majority German, Irish and Polish.

Historically, Chicago Lawn is infamous for the August 5,1966 march led by Dr. King and the Southern Christian Leadership Conference (SCLC), protesting open housing for Black Chicagoans. In rabid defiance to protestors, residents threw bottles, bricks and rocks. Afterwards, King stated, "I've been in many demonstrations all across the South, but I can say that I have never seen—even in Mississippi and Alabama—mobs as hostile and as hate-filled as I've seen here in Chicago."[12] In 2016, a memorial to the civil rights leader was erected in the park.

Miguel Alvarez is an elementary school principal (K–8) in Marquette Park—predominantly Black and Latinx today. He is in his late fifties and has worked for CPS for over two decades. He had previously served seven years as the school's assistant principal, but is now embarking on his second term as principal. We met in his office on the school's third floor. Filling the spacious room were two filing cabinets, a large wooden desk scattered with papers, and a black leather ergonomic office chair. There were nine security monitors stacked in rows of three on a table, each displaying different locations around and outside the building.

Recently, we caught a car pulling into our parking lot and guys getting out. Then, they backed up and they all took off [pointing to one monitor showing the rear car park of the school]. They were trying to get into my car. We were able to see the make of the car, the color, and we were able to see the shape of the guys, but the only thing bad about our system is that from a distance, it doesn't focus—not even on license plates. If the camera focused on moving objects, it would have gotten the license plates. All it got was the reflection, so we couldn't get the numbers.

Then, there was one child who had graduated from our school last year. He came back around because we have an outside portable basketball hoop that we leave up, take it out, roll it around, and we organize and play games. So, he thought it was going to be cool for him to be coming up here and playing with the guys. I was like, 'Oh no, this is only for those students who come to this school.' I said, 'Right now, you're on private property.' He got angry and came back on his bicycle and rammed into my car, dented the door and the spokes of his bicycle, and chipped the paint on my car. I had to get it repainted, you know the whole thing. But, we caught the incident on video.

You look at the monitors and you see if there are bodies blocking the halls. If there's too much activity, I can get on the intercom. But, I really don't rely too much on the cameras. I'm really out in the hallways and the classrooms. I like to think that my office is out there. I probably spend about half an hour a day walking the hallways.

Now, inside the school, we've seen kids fight. You know, the ones who are messing around. We recorded a young man who stole something from a student's locker. He said he didn't do it, but we had him on videotape. I told him to tell me the truth or we're going to call your parents and suspend you. But, he said he didn't do it. So, when his mom came up, we showed her the videotape of him going into the locker and stealing.

Just two years ago, we had a toilet overflow and flood the bathroom. So, we typically have to watch the activity of students around the bathrooms. There aren't any cameras inside the bathrooms, of course, but we can keep a close eye outside with security guards and custodians going in and out of the bathrooms. If we're watching the hallways and we know there's two guys in the bathroom and it's already been five, ten minutes, and they haven't come out, then we know something's wrong.

One time, we did catch one student humping another student in the boys' bathroom. He was taking his pants down and doing special things for the kids. So, the bathrooms need to be secured all the time. Parents are always being concerned. We just don't recommend you to go to the bathroom by yourself when you're a kid. There is always some kind of monitoring. What I prefer is that the teachers monitor bathroom breaks. But, even that can be a very difficult situation.

Outside of cameras, we don't have metal detectors or archways because sometimes they're hard to constantly supervise. When I was administration in CPS's downtown office, I would visit schools, some of them were manned and some of them were not. So, you could easily walk around the detectors. To be vigil at the door from morning to afternoon is difficult.

We used to have lines as a security measure. If you heard that somebody brought a knife to school, our security personnel would take that seriously and line up everybody that we had information on. Now, when students fight, I'll get right in the middle of it. But I feel more confident that my security guards are there to help me out. They deal with security, but they're also here in other modes. They check in with the young men who go to the school. The principal issue, for us, is a matter of teaching our kids how to act properly, have self-control and make good decisions. It's about promoting role models.

We wear uniforms here—a white shirt, navy blue bottoms. Students had problems with the white shirts at first because some boys would wear them and they'd get really dirty. And then, the parents had a hard time keeping them white. So, I put it to a vote two years ago and we changed to royal blue with our school insignia. Everyone liked that.

The kids like the association that they have with their school and they're really buying into that. And, it's not school uniforms for just for the sake of protecting students. The cameras are more about that. The uniforms are more about kids having pride in their school. So, they'll want to come to school and want to behave well. And, we're giving students rewards for that called, 'Tiger Bucks' that they can use to buy prizes.

Since becoming principal, we did have to do a search and seizure *once*. We had a little girl with drugs on her. It turned out that she wanted to impress a boy. She was in sixth grade and the boy was in seventh grade. Interesting thing was that when all of this conversation came out, and the police were here, the girl implicated her father because that was her father's stuff. I don't know where the police took it after that.

Our kids have insecurity about the neighborhood and about their community. I think they bring that feeling into schools partly because they probably have to walk back to their home, and they don't feel safe walking back. We did a survey and when they were asked questions about their security and safety they were responding to what I believe is not isolated to a building, but how they feel in general. I'll share the results of that survey with you later.

A good number of students thought that security was necessary. And there were certain numbers that thought they were safe, but a lot thought that they were not safe. Those were mostly in the upper grades. I think it's probably because they're facing harassment from other kids at school, plus in their neighborhoods from gentrification.

Our children come from various parts of the community around us. Some come from the east side around Commercial and 72nd Street. Some of them live at 76th and some from around here, so they're all coming from different parts. We have a lot of parents who have good jobs. They're mail persons, drive buses, etc. But, we do have some parents that are in extreme poverty. I mean, all of our parents are qualifying for free lunch, but not all are in extreme poverty. It's just where some of our kids are coming from, it's not safe.

We have a public park real close by and we have kids that are coming from the neighborhood who may have issues with some of those people in that park. So, at any time, either early in the morning or at dismissal, we're really sharp out there to make sure that kids go straight home and that they don't have interactions with some of the people in that park. All of my career service people, my security people and myself, we go out there because it's all security.

I think security measures are a deterrent. We haven't had many problems in a while, so I think that it has deterred. There are some schools in communities like ours that don't use much security measures and there are a lot of schools that do. But, I think it's where you put your priorities, how you spend your dollars. It's just a matter of having a priority. If you had to choose from buying books and buying a security camera, you would buy books. But I think part of it also is the security. When we opened this year, we spent a lot of money on computers and equipment, and wanted to make sure that all that stuff didn't just walk away. We had to protect the property, as well.

We do need to have better use of cameras and of observation equipment. I think that you can use it for safety reasons in the classrooms. I tell my teachers make sure students are not in the closets because for that moment they're out of sight things that can happen. So, that's a security measure that no one's at liberty to just go to the bathroom or to leave the classroom.

An underused security measure, I believe, is building a good rapport with parents. I'm not in the community where they're at. So, if anything is happening, I go through the grapevine. The information goes around and then it comes to me. That's the power of having a good relationship with your parents. If you're open to that, I think it's a good way to know what's going on in the school and in the neighborhood.

The year before I became principal, there were 175 suspensions. And last year, when I took over up to now, we had 35 suspensions. Part of my thing is that being we're such a small school, why just suspend kids without following it through with value clarification? You know, helping them understand why they're being suspended and then, what they're going to do after that. You know, you made a mistake—fine. All right, it costs two days suspension. But let's come back and talk about what if you were in the same situation, what would you do differently?

I don't want students to repeat the same thing over. So, I spend the extra time to do that dialogue with the kids. Believe me, they may still mess up. But if you ask them, they'll tell you exactly how they feel. I think, in time, that's what builds our real character. It's less about cutting them off and putting them out of sight, but more about getting the value clarification. Sure, you talk to kids and what goes in one ear comes out the other. But, if you repeat it, be persistent and keep on doing it, expect that they will have the power to make choices and that they'll make the right one.

September 2007

"I'm fixing to put them all on blast too."
QUINCY WASHINGTON[13]

North Lawndale, near Homan Square, is a west side neighborhood where Quincy Washington grew up. He is 17 and a senior at Zapata. He stands at 6'2", but seems taller given his lanky frame. He loves basketball and starts for Zapata's varsity squad as a shooting guard. Academically, Quincy struggles with math, but excels in science and literature. "I like the Harlem Renaissance. The poets from that time speak to me." Quincy has had numerous run-ins with school security and CPD ever since his freshman year at Zapata.

My school locked me up over some stupid stuff. You know, I'm walking to my division and this dude [student] I know come up behind me to ask me if I want to box. I told him, 'Go on cause you're only going to go tell your momma like you did yesterday.' His momma also approached me cause dude's little brother also wanted to fight me the day before. Me and his momma talked about it and I thought we had it squashed.

So, I'm walking to class and dude walk up behind me. My first instinct was to hit him. So, I hit him. Then, we got to fighting. His boys jumped in, then my guys jumped in, and there was a big ol' fight in the hallway. Then, the police came and locked us *all* up. They asked us why was we fighting. I said cause he ran up on me. He told the police we was fighting cause I thought he wanted my girl. Now keep in mind, dude was new here [Zapata], coming in, causing problems, plus I barely knew his girl.

The police finally let us go cause they felt the whole thing was dumb, especially dude. The police just looked at him like he was dumb. That situation caused 10 squad cars and two paddy wagons to come up here. Then I feel like dude's momma told the police to let us go because she's a security guard at the school. Dude feels like he can get away with stuff. That's why I feel that his momma might've set the whole thing up cause I just talked to her a day before. And if you really did talk to your son, then he's not fixin' to come to school the next day, early in the morning, and want to fight.

Another situation was with our dean of students who I had a recent conflict with. I was walking the hallways right. I was cutting seventh period cause I didn't feel like going. So, I see Nolan [a schoolmate]. I'm walking with him in the hallway. Then, his friend Darren walks up and he was like, 'Let's leave the school to smoke a square [cigarette].' I'm like, 'Naw, I ain't leaving the school for no square.' I don't even smoke squares. So Nolan's like, 'Okay, just open the door to let us back in.' I told him that I'm not opening the door either. Then, Nolan told Darren that he would open the door.

So they both by the door, right? Darren leaves out the school. I'm standing at the top of the stairs looking out for the dean. I'm looking both ways to see if anybody's coming. I see a lady teacher come past. I start talking to her, distracting her, right? So, Nolan opens the door for Darren and they coming up the stairs, while I'm talking to the teacher. She looks over my shoulder saying, 'I see all these dummies coming up the stairs' and waves down security.

Security guard comes over on the walkie-talkie. I told him I had nothing to say. He then get to saying our names. I told him whoever he was talking to just tell them to turn back around cause I ain't leave the school. So, when he was saying our name, that's when I heard the dean on his walkie-talkie. My basketball coach walks up and I'm telling him what happened and the dean cut me off saying we going to suspend him anyway. They didn't believe me cause of my history and I know I'm about to get five days [suspension]. That was my conflict with that dean.

The first time I ever been Maced was at this school. Police were spraying it when I walked past a fight. I avoided getting Maced my whole life until I went to school. Man, everybody starts covering their face. Police say they here to protect you, but they Macing us. That was about two weeks ago. It happened two days back-to-back. We went through six consecutive days of violence. The streak just ended last week.

I would say police are up at other schools on average every week maybe, but it's different here. The back of this building is operated by Chicago police and they crooked. They got their office on the whole third floor. I'm fixing to put them all on blast too. They was paddling mugs [students] up there last year. They was paddling me and my guys in there. We thought it was curtains for us. We had to fight security inside our own school. What you think about that?

And, when I come out of school, there's police officers and security guards right there too, standing on the corner. You can be there waiting on your ride and they be like, 'Keep it moving.' One time, me and my guys didn't move and security pulled out batons like they was about to start hitting everybody in sight. If we didn't move, I honestly don't know what they would've done.

September 2007

"They all look like babies."
SUSAN KLINE[14]

Susan Kline is an editor and a freelance writer for a Chicago-based newspaper that focuses on issues within CPS. Her work covers a variety of matters such as school funding, teacher unions, charter school expansion, school desegregation and youth unemployment. Susan also runs an after-school program for secondary-level students interested in journalism. Her class of 12 meets twice a week downtown at a private college. After reading one of her articles on CPS's decision to heighten school security, we sat down in her office to discuss the subject.

I've been researching school security specifically for the last two years, since Renaissance 2010 really took off. Before that, it was mainly community violence. One of the obstacles in doing school reporting is getting principals to call me back. [She giggles.] I had this data showing violent incidents per school that principals had reported to CPS. And so, that data may or may not be good data.

There's a lot of reporting issues in that data. But, I would guess that if you are seeing an increased trend, that's probably somewhat accurate. It's the reports that I've seen as decreased trends that I've questioned how accurate they are. Schools aren't going to over-report incidents of violence because it doesn't reflect that well on them.

If principals suspect that I have that data, they're not going to be that interested in calling me back to answer questions like 'What's going on with the school or what happened?' In some cases, and it's kind of funny, they'll say, 'The data doesn't reflect anything. Things are perfect here.' And I'm like, 'Well, why do you keep calling and reporting incidences to police?'

Schools tout all the things they're trying to do, but don't really acknowledge the underlying issues. So, sometimes you would have principals come to the phone and just sort of refute what the numbers say or you have a hard time getting ahold of them. And, it's not just principals. Sometimes, the security dean or the discipline dean won't call you back.

In other cases, some principals will come to the phone and they'll just say, 'Screw it' and talk to you. Other principals will tell you to call the CPS's Communications Department. The only reason why I don't like going through Communications is that I don't know how much they prep that person beforehand. You know, telling them say this or don't say that or don't say how much that is done. That's why I much rather catch the principal or keep calling until they answer the phone.

There was one principal at Schmitz[15] or maybe it was Corliss,[16] where he would not answer the phone or come to the phone. But, one day I called at all different times of the day and night with the hope that he would just answer. When he finally did, I started to ask these questions, and his initial response was, 'I don't want to talk the media. I never talk to the media.' But, I just kept asking him questions. So, he started answering questions, but sort of in a yelling way. You know like, 'Why don't you understand!?'

He sort of answered my questions, but he would always include the statement: 'I don't like the media because you guys twist things' and 'You don't know what goes on in my school.' And so, he told me what he thinks goes on in his school that I could use as a follow-up to my story. Sometimes you have to be a bit persistent. If you can just get a principal on the phone, most times they can't help themselves but to talk.

I'll tell you about a story that I'm working on that's coming out. I've been sitting in Dewitt High School[17] for a couple days a week now.

So, I'm sort of there when things happen and I kind of get both ends. On one hand, sometimes I feel like there's too much security on some of the little things like a lot of kids getting hollered at because they're wearing their hoods up. Are these little things worth kicking a kid out of school because he has a hoodie on? I don't know. They [security] say they can hide a gun in their hoodie. Sometimes the security officers are not really respectful of students and so it exacerbates what might not be a big incident.

Even with teachers, students feel they are being disrespected and so they respond with anger, which leads to their suspension. Certainly, you hear about these incidences, but you don't hear about them on a daily basis. I haven't seen a lot of teacher-student disputes. Mostly, I've witnessed what seem to be fights between kids who are upset with each other for individual reasons. They [students] say it's nothing to do with gangs, but just between kids they don't know and who are new to the school. I think it's also just young people not being able to express themselves in a way that adults can hear them, and then they get into disagreements.

As far as the other side of security goes, I'm sure you can get a gun into Dewitt. And, I'm sure kids are getting guns in there. Everyone walks through security. The thing goes 'Beep, beep, beep' all morning long and nobody stops anybody. If they were to stop all the kids that beep, they'd be there all day.

So I think those metal detectors are a façade. I don't think they really create safety. CPS's Office of Safety and Security told me they only confiscated six guns last year. So then, it's like nobody's bringing guns to school. Students get the message that you don't bring guns to school. I think that if you're inclined to bring guns to school, you can pretty much get them through.

The detectors aren't so much about safety as they are about control. I think it's sort of this inability to really figure out how to get kids to just come to school and behave, without having some of these artificial measures. You hear principals say that it's a very small group of kids acting out, and I actually really believe that. Even when you go to Corliss, there are tons of kids who come to school each day, put their stuff in their locker, try and go to classes, try and get what they can from classes, and go home and are not into fighting.

Then, there are some Dewitt kids who are just clowns. If they were in New Trier,[18] they'd be criminals. But at Dewitt, people would just be like, 'He's a clown, but he's not menacing.' No matter, something like that can get you kicked you out of school. A lot of what kids do is for attention. It's not like they're trying to be this menacing image. But, some of principals feed into this image and they're like, 'These kids are bad and we're a bad school and everything is so rough and this and that.' So, I do think it's a façade.

On the other hand, I think that there are underlying issues that these kids are dealing with that CPS schools don't tackle well enough and therefore it results in kids having more outbursts. The teenage years are hard enough. Forget the fact that you're in a new neighborhood and school. Your mom's not around or your dad's not around or you're struggling with all these things.

Then, you come to school and your teacher is being insensitive because she's got 35 kids in the classroom and she can't deal with your attitude today. The student has an outburst and there's really no one there to say, 'What's going on with you?' The response is 'Just get out of school' or 'Why would you want to bring a gun to school?'

Most of these kids know who the bad kids are, the kids with the guns, the ones new to the area or the ones in gangs. But still, I don't think schools do enough to ask questions like, 'Why are you doing this or what is broken in your world that you act this way?' Nobody really asks those questions.

Sure, when it comes to police, there are dangerous environments, dangerous neighborhoods. If we were to take away these things, some schools might erupt immediately and people worry about that. I don't think it's true that it would happen, but I think people just don't know. And, I think a lot of policing has to do with this public relations perception that we're doing something to prevent Chicago violence and crime.

Cameras and detectors are those obvious things you can do to show that you're doing something. You know, it's almost like the airport. We're not going to deal with the fact that a lot of people want to blow us up, but we'll make sure we go through security, so we'll all *feel* that we aren't going to get blown up.

I think some of the kids will actually say that because of the police presence, because of the cameras, because of the security measures, it actually indicates to them that they are in an unsafe place. In a safe place, you wouldn't need this stuff. Now maybe, as Mayor Richard M.

Daley, I look at them and I say that I'm creating a safe environment because I'm providing the police. Even a parent might say that their child is safer because the police are there. But then again, you have this sort of layer of distrust with the police.

I spoke with a parent from Crane[19] and she said that there are four cop cars sitting on each corner outside the school every single solitary day. Does that make her feel safe? Well, it makes her think that her son is getting harassed by the police every day after school. Is it good for the police to be there every day? If I see something wrong, I could tap a police officer on the shoulder. But to some people, who aren't little White ladies, it might not be the same thing. Police might not indicate the same level of trust or safety. It might actually indicate a level of danger.

When you talk about security measures or security guards, I think there are two layers to that. I don't know if you've ever been at a school when the kids are coming in. The guards are hollering at those kids, 'Get your hands out of your pockets!' 'Take off your hats!' 'Take off your hoodies.' There's just all this screaming and commotion.

One girl I interviewed from Dewitt says that she feels stressed out before she even gets to the classroom from the school being so intense and people hollering at you about clearing the hallways. It's not like, 'Excuse me, young lady. Can you please make it to your class?' A lot of the guards use curse words like, 'Get the fuck out of the halls!' as they walk down the hallways. You're sitting in class, trying to do your math, hearing this. How do you focus on what you're doing?

On the other hand, kids don't like to go to schools where there are a lot of fights. Nobody likes to go to a school if the word is two gangs are going to be fighting after school. That can also be stressful. I mean, it does scare kids because they know better than anybody that there's some truth to the fact that you can get shot by mistake just walking down the street. Kids are scared about that. Guards might be able to stop that kind of violence inside of schools, but the problem is that students have to leave the building and you can't make the whole neighborhood safe.

The girl from Dewitt is actually part of the Mikva Challenge.[20] She was a good interview and what she said really made sense. I guess, at Dewitt, the principal has taken the approach of kicking out the really bad students. Though you wouldn't find it in their school expulsion data or anywhere else, my sense is that the kids have been kicked out. The girl says that those students don't always go home. She says when you get to 95th Street, which is where they catch the bus to get home, the kids that got kicked out are there with nothing to do all day.

So, while you made the school a bit safer or it feels a little different, what do you do when you walk to the bus stop and those kids have been stewing all day, bored out of their minds, and are looking for some excitement. You might have created a safer school, but you didn't change the community. Students are like, 'So what, I'm not going to get shot in school. I'm going to get shot at the bus stop. That's nice.'

If there's any connection they see between school and community violence, it might be that order is more important than learning. I know this girl named Sadia. She actually works for my program and has done some articles for me. She was telling me about a crazy incident, where some kids had gotten into a food fight. The teacher hollered at one of them and told him to sit down. The kid got mad at her and he wound up being taken out of the class by police, put in handcuffs, and taken out the school.

We see so many people taken away in handcuffs that it doesn't matter. I think for many of us it becomes a common assumption. But, I could tell that the arrest really bothered Sadia. It was a kid that she knew. He wasn't a bad kid, but was like the offender of the moment.

This idea of police coming into schools and taking kids out in handcuffs has to change you. I'm not exactly sure how much because I'm not a psychologist. But, it has to change how you're viewing the experience of school as being this lively place where you might learn or where you might make friends or where you have some sort of socialization. Then, to go to school and see this kid being put into handcuffs and taken by police sort of reiterates all these messages that we send kids about how society looks at them.

A lot of kids already feel people see them as potentially a dropout or potential inmate. Then, they go to school and it's like a police state. Instead of dealing with a food fight and getting a slap on the hand, a kid wound up getting taken by police, handcuffed and dragged out of school. I mean, my God, what does this say? I guess it says, 'Hey, everybody thinks that you're dangerous and we're going to treat you like you're dangerous.' I think kids come out of that with a lot of negative impressions about schools and questions about their abilities to be in other situations and who they are outside their neighborhoods.

I think about how this happens at upper- and middle-class CPS schools. I know Andrew Johnson has a metal detector, but it's not used. Another one I know also has a nonworking metal detector, plus you don't even have to sign in. I completely think that society is saying that these kids aren't dangerous. We don't have to treat them like they're dangerous. The dangerous kids are somewhere else. That's a class issue, but it's also because of the images that we are fed.

If you hear there are always shootings in one place, then you'd be nervous to go there and you'd be nervous about the people there just because that's what you've heard or you're not familiar with. If you've heard that these kids are nice middle-class kids, they don't bring guns to schools, they don't do bad things, and they're going on to college, then you say we don't have to worry.

I really think the same things are happening in both places. Kids are getting into fights and people are getting into scuffles. Teens are teens by and large. This is the difference—one of the biggest fights at Corliss last year was over a prom date. It was a girl fighting another girl because she was pissed at this guy who went with another girl. You go to Andrew Johnson and the same story is about a girl mad because of a boy, but it's a display of emotion, not terror. They get into trouble and they're like maybe they need some counseling or a psychiatrist. At Corliss, it's a two-week suspension.

It's about the images we're fed and what kids internalize. You hear them say, 'I'm ghetto. I can fight.' It's like a badge of honor. At the same time, I don't think these kids are worse kids than the ones getting into fights at other schools. People look at some of these kids and say that they're so dangerous. I look at them and they're little bitty babies. They're not menacing. You go to the discipline office at Corliss and you're like, 'These are your bad kids? They all look like babies.'

I've even spoken with parents and community members. I've had some very interesting experiences. I remember I was at Crane's freshman orientation. I just happened to be sitting at this table with these two moms and they were just kind of talking about how bad the school was. They knew the reputation, but they felt like it was safe. They did worry though. One of them said, 'My child's not going to do any after-school activities because I have to pick them up at 2:15 sharp. I have to get them home because they can't take the bus. We live in a bad neighborhood and I'm not doing that.' We had a good conversation about Marshall and what changes they'd like to see.

I had another experience with an organization called Community and Family Issues or C.O.F.I.[21] They are really, really pushing against this idea of quick suspension and expulsion. They mainly talk about elementary schools and not as much about high schools. It's very interesting too because there was one incident where a high school was trying to move into an elementary school.

You'd listen to the elementary school parents and they're like all these high school kids are gang members and they don't want them in their elementary school. Now, forget the fact not everyone would agree to put a kindergartner in the same school as a ninth grader—you know, for other reasons—but that we know these kids are the bad kids. So, how much people sort of internalize societal images of themselves is interesting.

I think parents are just worried more about community issues. Most feel pretty safe with their kids in school, but worry more about their kids leaving school. I don't think they worry that their kids are going to get hurt in school and I don't think they used to worry before all these school closings and security measures either. I think that the idea has always been that while you are in school, you should be fairly safe.

The changes I would make to all of this, I think, is sort of a simple thing where we would have some community organizations go into schools and work on social-emotional issues with kids. Youth Guidance[22] has some programs that I've observed and they seem decent. I observed them at an elementary school in Englewood and it seemed like they were doing a nice job with the kids. They also have a program at Dewitt.

You know, there's a lot of politics involved in those kinds of programs because there's an emphasis on outcomes to get funding. They usually don't want to take the hardest kids who need their support the most. They want to take the kids they know will succeed, so they can say, '100% of our kids went on to graduate or 100% went on to do this or that.' But they know. I mean, you talk to the director of Youth Guidance and she'll say that there are kids out there who need us more, but we are sort of caught in this bind. At least we can rethink about the way we fund schools and organizations and how we can give them the ability to work with the hardest cases. It's only 10% that are really causing the problems, but there's a disincentive to not touch those kids, and those kids are just kids.

School violence sounds like such a menacing thing. There are schools that I think need to do a better job of figuring out why it is that they are not able to keep their fighting down or why some students fear they'll be in trouble with police every ten minutes and handcuffed.

At the same time, we have to keep it in perspective. Some people lose perspective and they start thinking that there's this horrible world out there. It's not really that horrible. I used to laugh at my brother who used to drive out of his way so he wouldn't pass through Cabrini-Green.[23] He heard all these bad things and I told him that it's not like constant shooting. When people drive to my house on the south side, they get this impression that it looks like a war zone. I mean come on. No place in Chicago actually looks like a street in Baghdad after a bomb went off. When you give that impression, you have to understand what that says about the people living there.

We spend 55 million dollars in Chicago Public Schools and much of that is based on fear of the kids we're trying to educate. Millions of dollars for security cameras, metal detectors and motion detecting sensors. We're spending so much money on this stuff, but does it really change the scenario that much? I don't think it does. Sometimes you hear somebody say, 'Now, I can catch the guy that pulls the fire alarm because I have a camera.' Yes, a pulled fire alarm can be disruptive, but it just seems like we're spending so much money for a camera to catch the kid that pulls the fire alarm. Maybe we should ask the kid why he keeps pulling the fire alarm.

November 2007

YEAR 2007:
QUESTIONS, REFLECTIONS & RESOURCES

Questions/Reflections

Imagine attending an institution of learning on a daily basis, where your mind and body are constantly surveilled along with the imminent probability of being punished for the slightest infraction—cutting in a lunch line, bringing nail clippers to school, or using an asthma inhaler. What kind of "lessons" might you learn within an environment of punitive social control and how might those around you—students, teachers, school staff, parents—respond over time to such conditions? Would they advocate on your behalf or aggravate your situation?

It was apparent from participant interviews in 2007 that not only was CPS deeply relying on zero tolerance policies—their remedy for community violence in the wake of gentrification and school closings—but also how these measures were in actuality a reflection of the broader society's incessant judgment and criminalization of black and brown skin—particularly young males. This dehumanizing treatment only pushed young people and Communities of Color further into political, economic, and emotional spaces of marginalization, isolation and invisibility.

Substantive takeaways from what is discussed by participants in this section are not just normalized school surveillance and compliance, but also the lack of alternative, more informed and compassionate processes for handling perceived youth disruption. Susan Kline makes an insightful comment in questioning outward student behaviors: "Why are you doing this or what is broken in your world that you act this way? Nobody really asks those questions." So, allow me: Why was CPS, as well as local politicians, constantly focused on the what of student actions and not the why and its root causes?

An added element to consider from these interviews, which was mostly raised by students, is the desire for less institutional control and greater institutional care. Aubrey Bell, for example, calls for hiring more teachers and social workers because: "There are so many kids that fall through the cracks and people don't see it. They just brush them under the table."

No doubt, school leaders and legislators must be made aware of the disturbing effects of racism on Black and Latinx peoples, as these communities at present have a higher than 50% risk for experiencing a healthcare facility closure (hospitals, clinics and pharmacies) than those in predominantly White affluent areas. This is a public policy issue yet to be addressed.

Although many young people, as well as adults, have come to accept the dominating nature of punitive policies, there still subsist human modes of conflict. Examples come in the form of youth disobeying teachers and school rules or an overall questioning and petitioning of authority for more lenient disciplinary measures.

As early as 2019, district and state officials across the country have been rethinking the negative impacts of hyper-discipline and policing inside of schools. Local and national reform of this nature has required representatives to entertain two opposing thoughts: How might schools in an era of extreme gun violence provide safety, while simultaneously creating ethical and caring spaces for learning?

In most recent localized efforts, there are some Chicago local school boards that have initiated plans to remove school resource officers (not police) from their buildings. With respect to these budding endeavors, I contend that educators, parents and politicians must avoid the trap of distinguishing between police and SROs who show violent responses towards youth and those who swear they serve and protect schools. This is a false distinction. The problem with school and community policing is not one of an individual officer's "do-gooder" deed, but rather a much larger, systemic issue tied to the long institutional history of policing as a force to protect public and private property boundaries and to control what is perceived as dangerous low-socioeconomic groups.

Put another way: White supremacy isn't about 1 or 100 bad apple cops in a barrel. We have to recognize that the barrel itself is rotten, and it doesn't matter what "good" cops say or do—the system itself is corrosive. The historical and structural legacy of American policing is founded on the specific intentional abuse of Peoples of Color—going all the way back to slave patrols in the 1700s, the enforcement of Black Codes in the 1800s, and Jim Crow policies during the 19th and 20th centuries, following up to the present with senseless police murders of Black and Brown peoples across this country.

If local, state and national leaders are genuinely invested in working with community folk to disrupt systemic racism vis-à-vis school and community policing, then another question that must be engaged and positioned at the fore of policy deliberations is: *How might we build healthy and safe communities of mutual respect without policing and what institutions are required to meet this goal?* I believe that by sufficiently addressing this query first, arguments around the utility of police in Black and Brown neighborhoods will not only become redundant, but also nonsensical.

Below, I offer a number of suggested books, journal articles, websites and other resources for advancing our thinking on school safety, the use of police in schools, and challenging racism and multiple methods for supporting the well-being of people throughout the United States.

Books/Articles

BURRELL, T. (2010). *Brainwashed: Challenging the myth of black inferiority.* Carlsbad, CA: Smiley Books.

CAVANAGH, T., MACFARLANE, A., GLYNN, T., & MACFARLANE, S. (May 2012). Creating peaceful and effective schools through a culture of care. *Discourse: Studies in the Cultural Politics of Education, 21,* 443–455.

DE LOS, REYES, E., & GOZEMBA, P. A. (2002). *Pockets of hope: How students and teachers change the world.* Westport, CT: Bergin & Garvey.

FUENTES, A. (2013). *Lockdown high: When the schoolhouse becomes a jailhouse.* New York, NY: Verso Books.

GIROUX, H. (2013). *America's education deficit and the war on youth: Reform beyond electoral politics.* New York, NY: Monthly Review Press.

HALL, H. R. (May 2019). What do Black adolescents need from their schools?: Knowing students' obstacles for building on their academic success. *Association for Supervision and Curriculum Development, 76*(8), 52–57.

LONDON, R. (2014). *Crime, punishment, and restorative justice: A framework for restoring trust.* Eugene, OR: Wipf & Stock Publishers.

McCAMMON, B. (2020). *Restorative practices at school: An educator's guided workbook to nurture professional wellness, support student growth, and build engaged classroom communities.* Berkeley, CA: Ulysses Press.

PANE, D. M., & ROCCO, T. S. (EDS.). (2014). *Transforming the school-to-prison pipeline: Lessons from the classroom.* Rotterdam, The Netherlands: Sense Publishers.

SHIRLEY, E. L. M., & CORNELL, D. G. (April 2012). The contribution of student perceptions of school climate to understanding the disproportionate punishment of African American students in a middle school. *Social Psychology International, 33*(2), 115–134.

TOCH, H. (2012). *Cop watch: Spectators, social media, and police reform.* Washington, DC: American Psychological Association.

Organizational Websites/Other Resources

Center for Community Change (*www.communitychange.org*) focuses on creating social movements in the best interests of empowering low-income people, specifically People of Color,

The National Association of Social Workers (NASW) (www.socialworkers.org) reports to have the largest membership of professional social workers in the world, with more than 120,000 members. NASW works to improve the professional development for all of its members and to create and maintain professional standards, and to advance sound social policies.

Teaching Channel (*www.teachingchannel.org*) offers videos and other resources for educators to watch, share, and learn new techniques to enhance their practice.

VOYCE [Voices of Youth in Chicago Education] Project (*www. voyceproject.org*) is centered on educational matters related to racial justice. It is led by students of color of Chicago, but also includes a network of other youth alliances from across the city.

Youth Activism Project (*www.youthactivismproject.org*) is a national organization focused on supporting the activism of young people across the globe. The organization connects with and assists young people, through online trainings and other resources, on how to organize and form meaningful collaborations.

YEAR 2007 NOTES

[1] A pseudonym.

[2] A pseudonym.

[3] A pseudonym.

[4] A pseudonym.

[5] A pseudonym.

[6] Named after Albert G. Lane, a former principal and superintendent, Lane Tech College Preparatory High School was founded in 1908. It is a public four-year selective enrollment magnet high school located on Chicago's north side in the Roscoe Village community. Soon after the launch of Ren 2010, Lane Tech reported a number of violent incidences to the district mostly related to "gang activity" in and outside of the school at the time.

[7] Founded as the Home of Mercy in 1886, Swedish Covenant Hospital is a nonprofit teaching hospital located on Chicago's north side. In addition to physiological healthcare, they also provide child development and physical fitness services.

[8] A pseudonym.

[9] A pseudonym.

[10] Bronzeville, also known as the "Black Belt" or "Black Metropolis," is located in the Douglas and Grand Boulevard communities on the

city's south side. Bronzeville stretches east and west between the Dan Ryan Expressway and Lake Shore Drive, and south and north between 39th and 36th Streets. Rich in Black history, Bronzeville is considered Chicago's version of Harlem during the Harlem Renaissance and was called "home" by many famous Black Americans such as Louis Armstrong, Gwendolyn Brooks, Bessie Coleman, Ida B. Wells and Richard Wright. At the time of this research, gentrification was already underway in Bronzeville.

[11] A pseudonym.

[12] *The Autobiography of Martin Luther King, Jr.* (1998). Clayborne Carson (Ed.). New York, NY: Intellectual Property Management and Warner Books, 305.

[13] A pseudonym.

[14] A pseudonym.

[15] A pseudonym.

[16] George Henry Corliss High School, known as Corliss High School, is a four-year CPS secondary school located in the Pullman neighborhood on Chicago's far south side. Today, Corliss shares its campus with Butler College Preparatory High School, a public charter school. The Pullman community is named after George Mortimer Pullman, an American engineer and industrialist who designed and manufactured the Pullman sleeping car. The area is the nation's first industrial planned community.

[17] A pseudonym.

[18] Founded in 1901, New Trier Township High School, in District 203, is a comprehensive public, four-year high school in Northfield and Winnetka, Illinois. The school is approximately 16 miles north of Chicago, serving about 4,000 students from Chicago's North Shore suburban communities of Glencoe, Kenilworth, Northfield, Wilmette, Winnetka, and portions of Glenview and Northbrook. The school, sharing community demographics, is roughly 80% White, 8% Asian, 4% Latinx and less than 1% Black, as of 2017–2018. In that same academic year, New Trier spent more than $15,000 yearly per student, which was nearly double the state's school funding average.

[19] Crane Tech Prep or Crane Tech High School, now called Richard T. Crane Medical Prep High School, is a public four-year medical prep high school located on West Jackson Boulevard in the near west side community. According to CPS statistics from 2011 to 2012, the school was graduating only 48% of freshmen within five years and only 5% of students were meeting or exceeding state standards, compared with the district's average of 28.8%. The dropout rate that year hit 29%, compared with a 7% average. In November 2012, CPS announced plans to phase out Crane, and the school became a medical preparatory high school, partnering with Rush Hospital, City Colleges of Chicago and the University of Illinois at Chicago.

[20] The Mikva Challenge is a youth development and civic education organization that was established in Chicago in 1997. Since then, it has become nationally instituted with additional sites throughout Illinois,

Southern California and Washington, DC. Named after former White House Counsel, Judge and U.S. Congressman Abner Mikva and his wife Zoe, the organization focuses on youth community problem-solving, youth electoral participation and youth policy-making.

[21] Community Organizing and Family Issues (COFI) is a nonprofit organization based in Chicago. It trains and supports more than 4,000 low-income parents, mostly mothers/women of color, to be leaders in their schools and communities.

[22] Youth Guidance was originally founded in 1924 as the Church Mission of Help and later, in 1962, took on its present title. Today, the nonprofit organization is major provider of outcomes-driven and capacity-building programs that operate in more than 100 Chicago Public Schools, serving approximately 11,000 youth and their families, across the city of Chicago.

[23] The Cabrini-Green Homes were a Chicago Housing Authority (CHA) public housing project located on the near north side of Chicago. At its residential peak, 15,000 people, predominantly Black, lived in the development. Constructed not too far from downtown, these projects sat amidst some of the wealthiest neighborhoods in the city. Over the years, crime, gang violence and neglect created appalling living conditions for the residents. Cabrini-Green then became synonymous with all the problems associated with public housing in the U.S. The last of the tenement high-rises was demolished in 2011.

YEAR 2008

"Two to the chest and one to the head is the way we are trained."
CHARMAINE JOHNSON[1]

Officer Charmaine Johnson spent 11 years patrolling neighborhoods for the Chicago Police Department. She was recently injured on the job and is now an instructor at a police training academy on Chicago's Southside. Despite her current "desk job," she is still ordered to work areas that her supervisors claim, "require a little more deterrence." So, once a week, Officer Johnson patrols Chicago public high schools. Her location assignments vary depending on where she is needed most, which is usually in schools where incidents of student aggravated assault and weapon violence are frequently reported.

My detail is in CPS schools because violence has been on the rise in a lot of the schools. What we do [she sighs], and let me just be honest, for the first five hours is really nothing. A lot of us are pulled from our desks and we sit in a squad car reading books. Some people bring DVD players. The only thing we do is listen to the zone radio. That simply means that, wherever we're working, we can find out what's going on in a particular district. So, when children are released from school, if there's an officer in that immediate area that needs assistance, you radio in to them. Otherwise, I mean, officers are running errands and just all kinds of stuff.

The whole thing is that, for one day, I'm not in my office and I have a sort of freedom to do whatever I want. I just have to be here when the kids are released and make sure that I pay close attention to that.

Today, I was at Oral Roberts High School.[2] Last week, I was at Hyde Park Career Academy.[3] That week, we were actually bouncing between Hyde Park and Roberts.

On the way to Roberts, my partner and I were listening to the radio and you could hear one of the security officers, assigned inside the classroom, requesting assistance. There was a group of children standing outside the classroom door. I guess they were waiting for the other kids to come out. When that happens, it usually means they're looking for someone in particular and sometimes it's for a confrontation—a fight. Actually, that's what happened on our way to the school. A block down the street, a big fight erupted, children were running towards the fight and it required about eight squad cars to come and disperse everybody.

We didn't know what the fight was about because as we were approaching, you just see the children scatter. Usually, they kind of block the ones that are fighting, but when they realize the police are persistent about breaking it up, then everyone starts dispersing and you really can't see who was fighting in the first place.

Along with CPS security, there are on-duty, sworn Chicago police officers assigned to work the entire building of Roberts. You also have off-duty Chicago police officers there, but working in a security capacity. CPS hires them because they are the police, but they're not there representing the Chicago Police Department necessarily. They're usually just making extra money as CPS personnel.

Every high school that I've ever gone inside, whether it was in a police capacity or as a guardian for one of my nieces or nephews, I've always seen police present. It's probably because of the dynamic of dealing with young people who have tempers and will start fighting. You need to have an officer present because CPS personnel are sort of in a catch-22 when it comes to putting their hands on children, even if they're separating them from a violent altercation. It's documented, so it's not perceived that students are being abused.

There are at least two perspectives on what goes on at Roberts. According to what was told to me by my supervisor, who met me and my partner at the school, a student had brought a gun inside the building. He was going through the metal detector and it sounded. When it sounds, students are to immediately take their bag and put it on the counter and either security or the police officer present goes through the bag to make sure there's no weapon there.

According to the police, the young man pulled out a gun and then he ran outside. The chase ended up at one of the CTA [Chicago Transit Authority] 'L' stops. The young man allegedly turned and pointed his weapon toward the police officer, who then shot the student. He's still alive.

The other perspective comes from the media. The newspapers are saying that the student's mother, who was not present, was told that her son did not have a gun. It was explained to her by a teacher who was allegedly there. The metal detector did go off, but it was *not* from a gun. The teacher stated that she never saw a gun. When she turned, the next thing she knew a police officer was running after the young man and they ended up in the CTA station.

The young man was apparently shot in the back, stomach and buttocks by officers. I'm not really sure what happened after that. All

I know is that there was a gun involved and when that happens, they make certain that police are present.

I was at Crane High School on the west side a few weeks ago. The school has eight squad cars detailed to it every afternoon because of the students. They fight each other in the middle of the street and some are afraid that they'll get injured coming out of the school itself. Last year, the violence was so great that they were throwing students out the window, and they had to put chicken wire up to form a barrier.

I think gentrification and school closings have a lot to do with the violence police are seeing. Many students are angry. If you get the chance to talk to them—and they certainly don't want to talk to us because we're the police—occasionally you'll get a kid who will make the statement that they're angry.

They see these beautiful homes that are now being developed in the area and they know that they could never live in them because it's too expensive. Their thought is, 'Why couldn't anyone create something like that for us. Why does it take some White person to make our neighborhood look nice?' Those expensive cars, those beautiful homes, and they feel that the outsiders are coming in and taking what belongs to them because they've been there all along.

They're tearing down where these people live. Where are they supposed to go and what are they supposed to do? When the city and all these private realtors knock down public housing and build new homes, they're being highly selective about who they are letting in. There certainly isn't enough room for those who are displaced. Where do they go? And, with welfare reform, a lot of students and their families don't have the resources they're used to. So, you have people from Altgeld Gardens,[4] Rockwell Gardens[5] and Henry Horner[6] losing their homes and fighting over resources.

With changes in the community, even some of the ideals of teachers are changing too. Their whole thing is, you know, 'We can't keep going through this. I don't want to be afraid to walk to my car every day. I don't want to be afraid to come into my classroom. Police officers, we need your help.' I think that's kind of what's going on now.

Outside of gentrification, you also have bullying and street gangs. From the fight today, I didn't see them physically fighting, but it did involve two girls. There was one young lady who was walking back towards us. Her hair was disheveled and she was mouthing off a lot and kept looking over her shoulders. Normally, when things like that happen, it's a fight between two girls and it's usually something social—whether it's about a boy, a look that that someone else gave, or a comment that was made.

As far as the gangs, most of that business plays out in their own neighborhoods or around their homes. In the school, it does happen, but it's usually when someone has been picked on or whatever and it escalates to the point where someone brings a weapon. That's the interesting thing about it. It escalates to this level of violence where I don't understand what it is with these children.

You hear this whole thing about television all the time and I think to a certain degree that has a lot to do with it. Children are desensitized about violence and because they're playing the video games and they're seeing the videos and they're seeing the movies that they are desensitized and therefore they think that type of behavior is OK. 'Well, they did it on television and no one did anything' or 'You see what happened? They gained respect.' In the end, these young people don't understand that that's not the way things work.

As for police presence, I think we deter this kind of behavior. I know that's sort of an ambiguous stance but, it depends on the school. It depends on the type of students in the school. The students at Crane are different from the ones at Lane Tech. I mean, not just because geographically they're located on two different sides of the city, but even the way the students behave is a little different. I've seen the students at Crane behave more violently, and more vicious.

For example, this was about two or three years ago. The Crane girls' volleyball team played another team. I think it was a suburban school. The Crane girls got angry when they lost, so they beat the other team up. That's crazy to me. The police had to be called there to get those girls out of the locker room. It was just that violent. For them to do that, with parents and teachers present, shows a lack of fear of consequences.

So, the question becomes, why do students still fight if they know the police are there, right? It makes you wonder if our presence there is really needed. Our presence isn't just for the students. To a certain degree, we're not really benefiting the students. I think it's what we signify. Our presence there is to sort of give people the mindset that if you behave in an undesirable way, we're here and we will respond to it. But even then, we're limited as to what we can do. We can't just grab students.

Just look at the political and social atmosphere in the city of Chicago regarding police officers right now. That's another dynamic. People talk about police misconduct. When we go in to do our jobs, just to pipe things down, people immediately think we've used excessive force and all these other things.

Actually, I think we need to be more present. I think there is an underuse of security. To me, with the average amount of police presence that's in some schools, it's not enough to really have the type of impact that would be needed for the students to take us seriously. If they have 1,500 students in a school, what can 15, even 20, police officers do? If these children decide to really have a big revolt, what could we do? At best, we're a deterrent. For some students, we just get them to think, 'I won't do that in front of them' or 'I won't do that now.'

For the teachers who have to leave the building and go to their vehicles, they know the police are there and they don't have to worry so much. You'd be surprised by some teachers who won't go to the parking lot for fear of students. Students aren't just fighting each other. They're attacking the teachers too. That's been another reason for greater police presence in schools because students were jumping on the teachers.

You would think it would be different given the neighborhoods, but not that much. Back in the day, and I'm talking in the '80s, some CPS schools had more Whites attending it. They're predominantly Black and Hispanic now. I think because you have a lot of students being mixed up in all these schools, the schools are changing, even suburban ones. You still have some White children and even middle-class Black ones attending previously White schools, but the school has changed. I can't put my finger on it, and I can't really say what I have to say without offending anyone, but it's like you have this influx of Black students that have come in and they're doing absolutely nothing.

Once Black students start coming in, there's more fighting, there's more gangs. They bring all that in. Then, you have the principal and the teachers asking for more police intervention. They want that police presence there. People don't want to look at race, but it's a factor. You still have that large influx of White students there and their parents make it very clear: 'We want our children safe.' The perception is more police means that things are safer, that the environment is safe. Obviously, that's not necessarily so. But the perception is that I see the police, so I know that if I need help, you're going to help me. That's the belief.

All that said, I really think that our presence in these hard-core schools means absolutely nothing. How do you think I come to that conclusion? Well, I was sitting in a squad car last week and a lot of times I will crack open the window in case someone tries to sneak up on us, especially in our blind spot. There was snow on the ground, so if someone tried to sneak up on our side, I'd be able to hear them before they approached the vehicle. We do that a lot.

It had to be 50 yards away and I could hear a conversation that this group of kids was having. It was sexually explicit, graphic, and they were using a lot of profanity. I'm trying to look over my shoulder, but I really couldn't see them because we have this cage in the back seat where we keep the prisoners. So, as they began to pass us, I picked up the PA and I said, 'Young lady, do you realize I can hear every word you're saying, which means that other adults can too?' I do that sometimes to the kids to let them know, we're watching you and we're listening—not as just police, but as adults.

The student responded by telling me how to 'f' off and 'my momma don't tell me what to do. What makes you think you can?' She didn't care what I said. She had no fear, no anything. She and the other kids started cursing at us and we're sitting right in the squad car. There was no fear that I could see with her body language and the other people that she was with. I was sitting right there in the squad car. They were cursing at us and they were doing all of that while walking further and further away from me. They had enough sense to do that.

I do understand is that I'm perceived a little differently. When civilians visit these schools, they're a guest and they are perceived as that. Yet, the mere fact that I walk in with that uniform on, students are like, 'Oh, you think you better than me?' There's hatred in that, but it's not for me personally. They hate me because I'm Black with the uniform on. They hate me because there's a history of that with them. You find that out later on when you get into a conversation with kids. They've been stopped by that officer who has beaten them up. If they weren't beaten up, then police put some kind of dope on them or one of their family members. I mean just all kinds of stuff.

They profile me and I admittedly profile them. Like the day I had to go to Hyde Park High School. I mean, that's the school I graduated from. But, today and 20 years ago are like eons. Not only that, but I live about six blocks away from the school, so I'm watching the behavior of the students and seeing all this police presence. I'm sort of part of the problem when I'm the police because of where I live. When I go to these schools, it's something that's present with me and I recognize that piece.

Sometimes, it's how they look with the black hoodie covering their head. I mean, to me they don't want you to see their identity, yet they talk so much about their identity. I find that interesting. They wear those hoods and they keep their head down because they don't want you to see their face, but they want you to see them. That to me is an interesting contradiction that I see a lot with kids.

I'll never forget this. It was about four weeks ago. I had just gotten off of work and it was maybe 3:30 or 3:45 in the afternoon. I had to shovel the snow in front of my house and it's a short walkway that ends with a wrought iron fence. I noticed these guys going down the street. It seems to be the only time they want to work is when they can make some quick money shoveling snow. So, this guy sees me shoveling and this was before I had gotten outside the fence. He couldn't have been older than about 19. He was about two houses down from mine and was just standing there.

At first when I saw him, I thought he was going to keep walking, but he just stood there. I knew that the house he was in front of was vacant because the owner had just moved out and it was for sale. I'm looking and I'm looking and he starts walking towards me. For my desk job, I wear civilian clothing, but he had no idea that I had my gun on me. Even if I'm working in civilian dress, that gun is my tool for my job so I have to have it with me.

It was cold outside and I had my coat on, so he didn't see it. Then, I started getting this funny feeling, so I walked up my stairs and I started calling for my dog. I have a 95-pound German shepherd. As I walked up the stairs, I notice he's coming my way and I didn't close the door behind me. I wanted him to know that I was yelling to someone upstairs. When I turned around with my dog, he looked at me and just took off running—left his shovel and everything.

It was one of those instances where, you know, he sees me and I have on the little heels and stuff. I think he thought I was going to be someone's victim that day. I know that was his intent because what other reason would he have to approach me, and then I call my dog and he takes off running. What he didn't know is that he would have ended up with 15 rounds in his body.

Now, as extreme as this sounds, three years ago I went to Israel. I was sitting next to kids with AK-47s and they couldn't have been any older than 15 years old. In Israel, there's a requirement that all the children have to go to the army—*all* of them. Aside from that, I still saw them just being teenagers. I saw some of them smoking and having their little groups. The difference was that they were all disciplined.

My personal thought, from just that one visit, is that we have a problem in America. Our children live in this era of entitlement. We've given our kids everything and now they feel that everything should be theirs whether they've earned it or not. As a result of that, when you start taking things from them and you prohibit them from doing certain things, they rebel. I think that has a lot to do with the behavior of a lot of these kids. They're rebelling because they are not getting their way. I don't know. Maybe it's because someone is intentionally withholding something from them or maybe that they're crying out for help and that's the only way they know how to get our attention.

I do feel though that there is a mix of entitlement and disenfran-chisement with school closings and all that. I think that's an issue. Plus, we won't even talk about what's going on in these kids' homes. When they get to school, and they know that because of overcrowding and things of that sort, they're not going to get that personalized attention there either. So, they need some type of outlet. A lot of times they're so angry that misbehaving is the only way they can sort of release all of that energy. So there are places like Roberts and Crane and Hyde Park that do need more security. They are minefields waiting to explode because these kids feel like they've been trapped—they have nowhere to go.

We could have more security, but I also think teachers have to do their part. Besides police, who else is present to dispel the violence? I think that's kind of where the administration feels that things have gone. I found this interesting because when I go into the schools, I'm there just to do a building check and to talk to people in the office. I'm not there to discipline students. I'm there just to make sure things are okay, but students will look me up and down and keep walking. They know me, but there's something about children when it comes to meeting people in uniforms. The uniform creates a barrier. I may say, 'Good morning. How are you doing?' I'm opening myself up, but they don't hear me. They just see the uniform.

Students need some dialogue. They need an advocate, someone to say, 'What's your beef? What is it that you need? What is it that prevents you from talking to your teacher or your parent, or your principal?' But, they don't talk and they don't listen. Then, the teachers feel that the only thing they can do is bring people who represent control and power. If they just had a conversation with the kids, they'd see just how backwards that is.

I'm trying to see things from a different lens, not just as the police. There's not a lot going on in the classroom. I know that for a fact. Things may not be going well at home, but they're still showing up at school every day. They're asking for some type of intervention. I think we have to create an environment for that. That may mean that, even though you have this tenured teacher over here, she doesn't need to be interacting with these students because she isn't helping them. We need people who can kind of speak their voice like a youth advocate but, at the same time, serving in that teacher role. They would actually be assuming a dual purpose.

A lot of these kids don't trust the teachers. They have no respect for them, and they have definitely picked up that a lot of teachers don't care. It goes back to the uniform and what it represents for these kids. So, with all of those dynamics, it's no wonder they are behaving the way they do. I still say the video games, the sex and the violence they're seeing on TV, plays a big part of that. I can't compete with this girl wanting to be like Beyoncé or Shakira or this young man that wants to be like 50 Cent [she giggles] or Biggy Smalls or Tupac. A lot of them are shooting for these dreams and they don't realize that maybe one in ten thousand make it.

We know they have violence in their communities and they have homelessness. They have a lack of education and, for some, unemployment. I don't know what to say, I'm torn. The administration does nothing. They complain and want to pass the buck on to everyone else because of what's happening in the city. So, when things happen, you have us to serve a purpose as the police to provide security. We're not here to babysit. You have me in here as the police, so I am going to do my job as the police. I am not going to coddle this kid who has a gun.

The fact that this child has a gun and is pointing it at me, means they have the intent to use it. Usually, a gun is for taking someone's life. Guess what? I'm going to take his first. I hate to put it that way, but that's the way it is. We're not trained to maim. I am not trained to hit you in the foot or in the knee. Two to the chest and one to the head is the way we are trained. If you're an offender, I don't care if you're ten. If you have a gun, you're someone that has the intent of taking somebody's life. That's the thing that people don't understand. Security is about protection of life and property. If someone is going to use force to take property or life, then I am formally trained to prohibit that from happening.

October 2008

"I just want to know what's going on."
HALEY ROBINSON[7]

Haley Robinson is a parent of a student attending Andrew Johnson High School. She lives only a few blocks away from the school. Haley shares leadership responsibilities with the school's parent organization. In our talk, she voiced reservations regarding the use of security at Johnson. "I'm not used to seeing so many police officers around here. It's all a little disturbing to me."

I don't believe our security guards are CPS employees. I think that they're hired by another company. I don't feel they're specifically trained to handle this clientele. I think that possibly they're trained to handle maybe criminals or adults, not adolescents, who are very unique creatures, so to speak. The security guards are not trained to de-escalate the situation, make it calmer and even like a teachable moment where students learn to live together and get along together.

The problems we're having here are related to gangs—not all of it, but some of it definitely is. I know there's hostility against teachers, even physical force against teachers. Another parent has categorized them as incidents that happen at any school. So, there's gonna be stealing. There's gonna be bad language. There's gonna be pushing and shoving. It's those types of incidents. You know, when people think of this community, they don't typically think of those kinds of issues. I certainly don't think about gangs. I mean, gangs are the last thing that would come to my mind.

The problem is getting information about these things from school administration. They're unapproachable in terms of information and they guard it well—no pun intended [giggling]. It's only privy to certain people and I don't think we're [parents] are the people privy to that information. I don't feel like school matters are freely disseminated among families. If they release something in an e-mail or newsletter, the language is vague, very vague. 'Everything's okay' or 'Things are getting better.' The principal doesn't really offer facts, so it's not a true picture. It's a very, very gray picture.

As a parent organization, we're not really recognized as a part of something to help with whatever real security issues face the school. That has been my issue for a long time, in that the principal is the leader of the school. She sets the tone and I don't feel like she is setting the tone. There are all these different arms to help her manage her school. Whereas, the Local School Council (LSC) only handles fundraising and it seems like we're almost pitted against each other with that. So, I don't think the principal sees us as a helper at all. I think we're kind of annoying to her. That makes things kind of sticky.

The principal made an interesting point the other day when one of the LSC parents said, 'I feel like I don't know what's going on in this school. I don't get any information from my daughter.' And she said, 'Well, what do you want us to do? Send her home with something pinned to their shirt?' I mean, there is a certain level of responsibility that comes with being a teenager and attending a high school environment.

What I got from the principal's message is that parents and students need to communicate. I understand that. Students know a lot of inside stuff more than anyone. However, I believe that she [the principal] should tell us the truth. I think she should inform parents of things that aren't just about making us feel better. Even though talking to our kids is important, parents need official information.

When we had an ex-student threaten the school, I *heard* that on that day security guards and plainclothes police officers were in and around the school. When I dropped off my son, all I saw was a barrage of police officers, all in line. It would've been nice if I could have received a call or text or e-mail or something to be better informed. I didn't know anything until I came to the building.

At Johnson, we have different kinds of security for students. Freshmen have their own little like archway that they walk through. They have fire escape doors, but there's only one door that all students come in. Students are randomly searched before entering and, occasionally, they have to be strip-searched. My God, strip-searched. This is just removing a coat or jacket.

Recently, administration has asked for parents to get involved with doing security. Can you believe that? The point I made at our last LSC meeting was that if you want to get more parents involved in the school, start publishing the CAPS[8] report. Let the parents know what's going on in the community and in the school and that will motivate them to come in. It's a good motivator.

In the absence of parents as security, Johnson has both police and security guards patrolling the school. We have seven security guards that quote 'belong' to the school, extra security officers and I think two to four police officers that ride bicycles.

I'm not sure that I or my son necessarily feels safer with security. My son is an 'under the radar' kind of kid. He blends in. He doesn't really do anything. So, in terms of him feeling safe, he's never made any really distinguishing comments about whether he feels safe or he doesn't feel safe. He's only made one comment about security guards and it was more positive.

I personally don't feel comforted by the type of security guards that we have here. I think they are too aggressive. Just because they're here, I don't feel like they're creating a safe environment. I feel like they're treating us more like a rigid institution. I know school's an institution, but more of like an incarceration type of situation. Why can't we just have a free discussion about the state of security here? Why are all these questions still out here? Why?

There was a problem with security guards when they came. I think three or four years ago. I learned this from one of my colleagues. She had a daughter that graduated from here. At the time her daughter graduated, the security guards were arrested for contributing to drug trafficking in the school. They had students bringing drugs in for them to sell or they would allow students to sell drugs in the school. The security guards knew which students were bringing the drugs in and they brought them in. That was fairly recent like four years ago.

This is what I mean by an 'incarceration' type institution. Doesn't what I said sound like prison life? Guards allowing drugs into an institution that they are supposed to be freeing from it? Guards even profiting from the trafficking. That's a mess, right?

I try to make some waves at the school about school security and what I hear. I try to talk to administration. I just feel like the principal is more sensitive to the well-to-do families of Johnson. They don't want to hear about police and drugs. They just want to know where IB is going on their European trip. My concern is, or my question is, 'Why don't we have school uniforms?' You know what the principal told me? She said that she didn't want to offend those well-to-do parents. Imagine that. What really matters most, I wonder?

We have such a big population of students and of course parents. There are some parents that really like the principal and some that don't. It's just because there are so many people. There isn't going to be everyone on the right and everyone on the left. I think there are some teachers who think she is the greatest. I talked to one of them last summer.

The principal had brought in a wonderful initiative. It was like every student who was taking a college admissions test would get a free practice test. It cost the school $7,000, and she was able to get it through the LSC. So, this teacher thought that the principal was doing a wonderful job in terms of the quality of instruction.

What about the police in our school? I think security influences the way the environment goes. I think that anytime you make something taboo to humans, it makes them want it more. If you tell me not to walk in the grass, I really want to walk in that grass. So, if there's security guards that are telling students exactly what to do and how to do it, it only makes them want to rebel against that. In the end, there needs to be compassionate authority. It has to be security guards that know how to deal with teenagers.

Security may be an extra set of eyes, but they're an authority figure. They are *not* to take advantage of their position of authority. They're not to use that as an advantage over the students. They just need to be an authority. But, it's the way that CPS is funded and the way schools set up their budgets. That's why there's so many overlapping roles. That's why you have substitute teachers being hired to be security guards.

Ideally, I'd like to have schools without security guards. We don't need them. We have to look at the students to know where they are coming from and what kind of support they need. Students have changed over the last thirty years. The families are different. Their financial status is different. If we need to have security or some an element of control and safety, then what are they here to represent?

It also starts with the principal. The principal dictates the atmosphere. Is she going to be a good communicator? Is she going to expect her faculty to be good communicators? And, is she going to be a leader? I just don't see our principal leading in that way. Parents, all parents, need to know security policies. They should know why security is being used and what that means. They also should know the security guards by name. Security guards should be on our website. I'm going to post their names and faces on our site.

If there is anything I would change about Andrew Johnson High School, I guess, would be to improve communication by making sure that the security guards are doing their jobs. How do I know that they're not doing what they're supposed to be doing? I don't know their job description. I don't know what she [the principal] has told them to do. They could be doing their job to a T, but I don't know it.

I do believe that security is necessary. It's just the world we live in now. My family takes more preventative measures living in the city than when we lived in suburban Michigan because we know it's a different environment. It's different because security is necessary in this urban type of environment. I just want to know what's going on. When and why do we need it?

March 2008

"Why is our school like the airport?"
JOCELYN RAWLS[9]

Jocelyn Rawls is 17. She is a senior at Robert Latimer High School,[10] located on Chicago's south side. Her academic interests are math and science. One of Jocelyn's life goals is to become a secondary-level teacher and help teens who struggle with core subjects like she has. "I just think there needs to be someone to help young, Black youth, who are incredibly smart, stay in school and realize their genius. I want to be one of those people."

Latimer High School closed in 2017 due to declining enrollment. It was a public four-year high school, serving over 98% Black students with less than 1% Latinx. Anyone external to the school's three-story brick building might mistake it for a police station with police cars, SUVs and paddy wagons filling its parking lot. Entering the school, there are metal detector archways, as well as X-ray scanning machines for book bags, purses and all other carryalls.

I think we have bad security. We have probably three security guards on every floor and the first floor has actual cops. The kids are pretty much out of control. I don't think they know the purpose of coming to school and what they supposed to do in school. So, I would say it's probably more money spent on security things than anything else. You know, instead of books for the kids, we're going to get some new security cameras. That's how it is.

We have paddy wagons outside. Two metal detectors at the front door when you first walk in. But, if you go through and they don't beep, security is still going to check you, especially the guys, head to toe. Even if they have to and make you take off things, they will do it. And, I understand. It doesn't happen often, but kids will bring in weapons. There was one incident where it was a fight between females and one of them got a knife into school and she stabbed one of the girls.

The police officers here are like the ones who patrol my neighborhood. It's them who supposed to be protecting us. But, if a fight breaks out the police will jump on you. The police will jump on you with nightsticks. Whatever they have to do, they will jump on you. They don't care if you're the one not fighting, or if you're bleeding, they will jump on you and they will arrest you.

Like, I've heard stories from my brothers and their friends. They could be outside minding their business and police will harass them. I mean, hit them. And, it's not like they can do something about it because first off it's going to be their word against the officer. Then, if they pull up their record, they'll find different things and that's going to count against them too. It's like your word is shot. Your word don't mean nothing against theirs. When it comes to African Americans, the police don't care.

There's been situations around here where kids will be getting jumped on for weeks. We have a police station up the street and all them cop cars outside, plus we have three or four police officers sitting on they butts in our school and they don't do nothing. Yet, right outside, kids are getting jumped. So, where are the police officers then? I bet as soon as the sun go down, every officer at that station will be riding around, patrolling, trying to find someone selling drugs or doing something like that. They're not there when *we* need them, but they're there when *they* think they need to be.

I feel like the police treat us like second-class citizens. Like they're trying to intimidate us and the whole point of them being in schools and neighborhoods is because they know that we're going to do something wrong and they think that we're going to fail. They put us down. So, I think that the whole act of having security around is about telling me and all of my peers, 'You're going to mess up so and we're ready and waiting for you.'

I think police in our schools and neighborhoods is abnormal. I'm the kind of a person that likes to go out and experience different kinds of things. In the summertime, I don't just sit around. I take college courses and I also visit my sister's college, Northeastern.[11] When I'm at those schools, I see the way they do things. There's not a lot of heavy policing. Then, I come back to my school, in my neighborhood, and I'm like this is not the way it really works.

I went out of town last weekend. I was at the airport and it was real busy. And, you know, airport security has to be top-notch because it's like the airport. You have to take *everything* off—your jacket, coat, belt, shoes. So, I'm looking around and the airport looks like my school. Like here I go through the metal detector every day and I have to give security my phone and take off my coat. And, why do I have to take off my earrings? It bothers me. You're treating me like a criminal.

You can go to different Big Ten or Ivy League colleges, but it's *our* school that can be compared to an airport. That's ridiculous. That tells you something is wrong, when your school has security like the airport. Why is our school like the airport? I know we have a few bad kids and some shady things happen, but why treat everyone else like they're terrorists?

The school and the alderman and all the top officials in this area need to come together and think of solutions that are going to help the neighborhood. It's not just about the school. It can't be just about the school. You need to help students, parents and businesses in the community. You need to do all of these things because we're all one, we're all connected. If one fails, the other fails. If one link is broke, you know the chain is broke. You need to fix it all.

All these security cameras and blue lights,[12] I want to say it's like a mental thing. If you're raised that way, the kind of background that you come from where you're used to violence and fighting, then it doesn't matter if there's a camera up or there's more security. It's like, you need counseling. You need help because you're not going to be afraid of some blue light or a police officer standing on the corner. You need help, so you can learn. A man standing there is nothing, you're used to it, that's your way of life, and it's common for you. I think schools need to look past security guards and get more into social workers.

The violence is there. That's absolutely true. You have students that go to the school like me that care about education, and then you have people that, you know, wander the halls every period. Sure the violence is there, but security is the Band-Aid. We still need to bring in counselors, people who take a deeper look into each individual situation.

Generally, the situations are all the same—you struggling, you need money, or somebody's parent is beating on them or something like that. But, we all got a different momma and a different daddy. I think it's all the same, but also different. And, I think that we need to stop covering these problems up and actually think of solutions to fix the problems. We need more counselors, but they keep firing them. Latimer used to have four. Now, we only have two—one for freshmen and sophomores and one for juniors and seniors. None of them know who I am.

I believe schools can move towards individual student care. It could happen, but that's not the direction we're going in right now. It's possible, but I don't see it happening. I'll graduate and be long gone before it does. And, that's perfectly fine for me because I'm fortunate enough to have outlets in my life, whereas others are not and it shows. When you're running through the hallways and you're jumping on desks and you're doing all kinds of abnormal things in school, it's something wrong with you. Nobody is looking at that. They're just going to say, 'Ah, this kid is crazy. Give them 10 days and run him out the school.' But, why is he on the desk? Why is he cussing out the teacher?

Instead of all the security, there could be rooms or offices where students go and talk with people. They can be old or young, but a person students can relate to that's been in their shoes. People need to realize that kids are not going to come out and say, 'I have a problem and need help.' You need to see and realize it and then institute initiatives to help them. While it's on them to seek help, some kids have to be pushed. It's a mentality, where everybody is not going to be that outspoken person to come and ask for help. Pride is going to get in the way, different things is going to get in the way. As an adult that's caring for me, you can take the initiative to see what's wrong with me because it's your responsibility, it's your job.

If students have people there to help, then they'll probably be more willing to listen and act better. But, if you got somebody who says, 'You get 10 days.' What does that mean? What's the student going to say? What are they going to do—go home for 10 days probably to a family who could care less if they have 10 or 20 days. It's a cycle. But with a counselor, instead of 10 days, you can meet with her 30 minutes out of the day, talk, and learn something before you make a bad decision.

Students could also look to teachers. I have some awesome teachers. A lot of them are going to leave though because of the way our school system is set up. It's not just our school, but CPS, period. It's dreadful, and a lot of them are leaving. The administrators at our school treat teachers like they're kids. I'm talking like yelling at them in front of us. That's disrespectful. Why would you want to work in an environment where you don't feel respected?

That's the difference between Latimer and a school like New Trier. Teachers get more respect. Students get more respect. New Trier gets funding from the neighborhood *and* they have families with money compared to a lot of kids at Latimer who don't even have a family. They're in foster homes or struggling to be in relationships with their family. That takes a toll. That's where the violence comes from, and the fact that we don't have nice houses or nice cars. We want that quick cash to get some nice shoes or whatever. So, to get that stuff we resort to negative things and I think that has to do with economics.

Money is the issue. Not necessarily how much my family makes or your family, but how much money a school has. Like, I could walk into my school and feel pretty good because everything's relatively new. For the most part, we've updated our old computers and stuff. But, I could easily walk into New Trier in the suburbs and feel a little ashamed about what we're doing here. They have more advanced, even better, computers and up-to-date books.

If you constantly come to school and books and walls are falling apart, it plays on you mentally. You have the same book since you was a freshman, now you a senior, and the facilities aren't up to date and you don't have access to good computers. These are real-life situations and this would do something to me mentally. If you don't care enough about my education to fix up my school and give me the right materials, then why should I care? That means that you don't care about me. Maybe administrators don't see it, but instead of security, kids need psychological help.

It really goes back to having a good school, teachers that care, a loving family and learning morals. Some kids don't have that. I've never thought because they give us these raggedy books that I'm not going to work. But, I think it's less about the school and more about the community and what's invested in it.

If you were born and raised in the projects and your parents don't have education, you might wonder, 'What's that going to do for me?'

And then, you're constantly being brought down. All that will make you afraid of failure. We're afraid that if we go out and do it all—go to school every day and work hard—that it's not going to work in the end. We won't be able to go to college or get that job, so it was work for nothing. We're scared. So, we all need someone to motivate us, to keep us going. Without that, what do you have?

February 2008

"They literally fight to kill."
PATRICIA WRIGHT[13]

Patricia Wright is nearing her sixth year of teaching in CPS. She specializes in English College Prep and Honors courses. From her youthful appearance and slender build, one could easily mistake her for a high school student. Her first two years of teaching were at Zapata. She later transferred to Mason Career and Vocational Academy[14]on Chicago's south side. In 2007, Mason expanded its attendance borders in order to take in displaced students from closed schools west and south of its locality. The idea was to give families more options, contingent upon where they lived. In 2008, Patricia earned tenure, completed her master's degree in Educational Policy and, at the time of our talk, was planning her upcoming wedding.

At Mason, we have quite a few security guards. We have two metal detectors at the main entrance of the building where all the kids come in. We have security cameras, but they're pointed toward the staircases closest to the fire alarms. The kids get wanded after they go through the metal detectors. That is, if they beep or if anything beeps, they get wanded.

We have a conveyor belt where the book bags go through, but I don't think it works all the time to be completely honest with you. I've seen it working, but I've seen it not working more than working. Last school year, we had to do a serious lockdown. There was a gun incident where one of the kids, he was freshman at the time, snuck a gun into the building. He called a friend to open the door for him. He just brought it into the school to play with. I don't think his intent was to hurt anybody, but he ended up shooting someone in the leg.

Now there's a lot more security posted at that particular area, where the kid got in and out. So, there's some entrances in the building where they've kind of beefed up security, but we've got so many doors that we don't really have the manpower to cover all of them. Those entrances have been a big problem in the past, but they have put more security in those particular areas. There are less kids coming in and out, but we can't really secure everywhere because we don't have someone to stand there all day long or a camera pointed that way. So, the kids still get in and out.

I guess the purpose of the security is to make sure that the kids aren't coming in with weapons, but I don't think it's a foolproof method. One of the problems that we have is that the kids, if they really want to get into the building and not go through one of the metal detectors, they just call a friend to let them into one of the side doors. And now, this is the first year that we've had alarms at the side doors, but nobody really pays attention to them. Even if the kid is already in and ran up the stairs or they ran out of the building, they were at such an angle that they were out of the camera's sight. There's not a whole lot you can do about it. If there's a security guard close by, the kids don't usually go to that door.

We also have two full-time police officers and they have an office. We have plainclothes cops that work in the building part-time. We used to have a lot of part-timers, but I think we only have a couple now. It's weird because I know of a couple more that are coming in at the end of the school year. It's just the timing. I know one is a new police officer and you have to work for the force for a certain period of time before you can work part-time at a school. So, I know that's an issue for one of them. I think the issue for the other was just like organizing the paperwork and stuff like that.

With the boy who accidentally shot another student in the leg, the school didn't immediately talk much about it. We wanted to talk, like the teachers wanted to know what happened, what was going on, and what the school was doing about it. We had a forum after it happened, but it was weeks after and I think it was to only pacify us in a sense. Teachers and students were there. Administration didn't really address the incident. They didn't say what happened. They didn't say how it happened or how it could have happened without somebody noticing how this kid brought a gun into the building. We never really got the answers we wanted from that forum and steps needed to make sure that it never happened again.

We had a professional development day shortly after the shooting incident, but it wasn't addressed the entire day. It was a general body meeting. We often have those at most of our professional development sessions. We start off the day with like a general meeting—all the teachers in the cafeteria with the principal and the assistant principals and it wasn't even addressed. Our principal and three assistant principals decided collectively on the topics and what was to be done on those days. Our principal usually runs the general body meeting, but the entire administration sets the agenda together.

After the shooting, I wasn't necessarily concerned about my personal safety. Around Mason, it was more like, 'Why aren't we talking about this?' I think that was from the teacher's point of view. It was more like we don't feel like the kids are safe. I don't so much worry about my personal safety as much as I worry about the kids. The kids need to know what happened. We [teachers] need to know what happened, so if the kids ask us questions we know how to address it because we have all the facts, instead of a lot of hearsay. Nobody really knew what actually happened. So, it was more of, 'Why aren't we talking about this,' especially since there had been a shooting in the parking lot just weeks before the classroom incident.

As for the parking lot shooting, it was neighborhood stuff. One of our kids got shot, but it wasn't by students that actually went to our school. It was some stuff from the neighborhood. Whoever it was knew that's where the kid went to school. They were arguing and it happened in our parking lot because our kids were running towards the school to be safe. It actually ended up being something that they had argued about in the neighborhood prior to the school day. I know it was something really trivial.

But then [heavy sigh], we had a shooting two weeks later in the school. The kid that shot another kid in the leg was in a science class, which poses a great danger seeing as how there are chemicals in the class. I mean, it's science. The shot could have made something explode and we'd all be goners by that point. In either case, it was like we didn't talk about it. Teachers felt, 'Why don't we address this because we don't really know about the circumstances that led up to the gun going off?' We never really got all the details, but the one that happened in the building, we didn't address at all. And, because it was so close to the parking lot incident, we were like, 'Okay, are we ever going to talk about this? Why do we keep avoiding it?'

I know a few teachers and myself talked about it with our students. We talked about whether they felt safe. I think, unfortunately, a lot of them blew it off because the kids knew that the gun was there. They knew that he had it and that he was showing it off, but they didn't say anything about it. He brought it to school to show his friend not to use, not to shoot someone for real, but rather, 'Look, my boy gave me this thing.' They were playing with it in class when it went off and he shot his classmate. The kids thought since he was just playing with it and being stupid, they didn't take it as serious as I think they should have.

Oh, and the media ate up the story. I mean, especially since they reported on the one that happened in the parking lot weeks earlier which wasn't even connected to the school. The person that got shot wasn't a member of the school, but the media connected it to the school itself. So, they were up at the school wanting to talk, but our principal didn't talk to them.

I think our security measures help in extreme situations. I mean, there seems to always be kids in the police office for whatever reason.

The police office is on the first floor. We see police presence more so throughout the building when there's been a lot of fighting going on. To be honest, I don't really think about police in the school now. It all caught me off guard when I first started working at Zapata.

I didn't go to public school when I was younger. I went to private school and we didn't have metal detectors. We didn't have police officers in the building. We didn't have security cameras, so it was a little off-putting at first just because, when you see that, you automatically think rough area, you know? Rough kids, rough whatever. After a while, I don't really think about it that much anymore. It's just kind of there. It's just one of those things. As for the students, I haven't really talked to them, but they don't really seem to be concerned about it either.

Last year, I think we had the most pulled fire alarms of all city schools—false fire alarms. Kids pull them so they can go outside and fight basically. Sometimes, it was gang related, sometimes it was just kids from different neighborhoods. We have maybe two major gangs at the school. Kids don't really talk about others. It's just two. But, some of them are actually in those two gangs and some of them are just like wannabes. They're all sagging, but it's cool. I get it.

Truthfully, I don't think students feel that security guards effect their learning or social interaction. They [students] just do whatever because they know they can. Security's there, but security's been there when they've done bad things and don't get in trouble. Sometimes it's just because the security's overlooked it or didn't follow through with any consequences. Of course, we lose credibility as adults when this happens. They [students] think, 'You made such a big deal about me doing this and you wrote me up, took me downstairs, cuffed me, but then I was back in the hallways a few hours later.' I don't know if this is a reflection of security or their training, but we have a lot of new security guards in the building this year that, in my personal opinion, are not effective by any means. They're a joke.

When a security guard stops a kid in the hallway, they're supposed to have passes to go to the bathroom. It's bad when the kids just are allowed to go to the bathroom and smoke weed or cigarettes. We [staff] keep telling them [security] about this, but it still happens. We keep telling them because it makes the whole floor smell. We report it, report it, and report it. We lock the door. What happens? Nothing.

A couple of weeks ago, there was a bunch of boys in the bathroom smoking. The teachers got so fed up that we locked the kids in the bathroom and waited until one of the deans walked upstairs so he could write them up because security was doing nothing about it. We locked them in the bathroom for two class periods [90 minutes]. We probably aren't really allowed to do that, but they're smoking weed in the bathroom and the security guard was okay with that. I mean, he just kind of brushed it off. He kept letting them in and out of the bathroom. And we were like, 'Stop letting them in and out of the bathroom.'

On a scale from 1 to 10, one being 'ineffective' and 10 being 'the most effective,' I'd probably give our security a 6 or a 7, depending on which part of the building they're patrolling. Overall, I'd probably give it our security a 4. There are certain areas of the building that are secured very well. The Achievement Academy is secured very well because it's a smaller, contained area. The areas of the building that don't have a lot of student lockers are secured very well. The side of the building that's on the second floor is secured really well, but that really changes depending on where certain security guards are posted.

We have some really good security guards and some really bad security guards. This year, they've been doing a lot of shifting of guards. Every two weeks they're moving around the building, which I hate because each security guard has their own style for handling the kids. Some are easy and pushovers and some aren't. The best secured areas are the ones with the more experienced security guards. One of our better security guards is on the third floor because he had surgery on his leg. Now, we have two security guards on the third floor—one on one side of the building and one on the other.

I think we have more security guards this year than we had last year. We have more inexperienced security guards this year than before. Administration increased the number of guards because more students new to the community were coming into Mason. But, the new ones are not properly trained. So, it's like we have less because more of them are not really effective. But, at the same time, we're putting more students in the hands of guards. That's a problem even from a teacher's point of view.

When we have our prep-periods or times where we can sit down with the kids, we can't because we have to fill out this sheet and we have to fill out that sheet. We have more paperwork as teachers and counselors, and the people that are the ones who truly nurture and look out for the kids can't because we lose time. All our work doesn't allow us the kind of time to build those relationships that kids need. I mean, we still do, but probably not to the degree that would be the most effective for a lot of them.

Just this year alone there've been about 20 CPS student deaths. Two didn't involve guns. Outside of a few that happen on school grounds, most were in their neighborhoods. But, that didn't stop CPS's CEO, Arne Duncan, from calling those who engage in such acts as 'Al-Qaeda,' which is an interesting way of framing youth as 'terrorists.' So, where do we go after that? She's a terrorist, but her grades are coming up. He's a terrorist, but he's on the basketball team. It seems to speak to the lack of compassion that we have towards kids, which has led to more CPS security without getting at root causes.

Without really addressing the reasons as to why violence is there in the first place, I think it's easy to overlook root causes. We don't have to actually put in the work to figure out why kids act the way they do. It's so much easier to just beef up security, put it in the security guards' hands instead of really sitting down and taking the time to talk to kids and figure out why they think violence is a necessary step. Actually, they're at the point where they don't just fight. They don't just argue. It's to the point where you bumped into me in the hallway, so now I'm going to get my crew of 20 people to come jump you when you're by yourself. They literally fight to kill.

Some of them only know how to fight in order to deal with conflict—any conflict. They fight at home whether it's for attention or they live in a rough area and you have to be tough to survive. I think they are always in survival mode and they don't know how to turn that off. And nobody's showing them how to turn it off. They don't see that you can solve a conflict without taking it to that level. You don't always have to fight. They don't know how to have a dialogue with someone.

When you get older and you're pissed off at somebody or get angry, or whatever, you can either let it go and say 'I'm just not going to deal with that person at all' and be fine with that. You could also talk it through and get it off your chest. You may still dislike each other after, but at least you got it off your chest. Students don't do that. They kind of let all this anger and frustration build up because they don't know how to express it. They don't have a healthy way of expressing it so it compounds into this aggression and fighting is the only way they know how to fix it or solve their problems.

I ask my students sometimes, 'Why don't you just talk to her?' They say, 'It doesn't work that way, Ms. Wright. It doesn't work like that.' And I'm just like, 'Why not?' For instance, we were talking today about a phrase that I put on the board: 'Revenge is the only way to get true justice.' So, many of my students agreed with that statement. I asked them, 'Where does revenge end for them?' They were like, 'It ends when someone dies.' I was like, 'No it doesn't because people are dying all over the place and revenge still exists. All revenge does is make more people upset and make more people want to act out in revenge. So where does it stop?'

We were reading *Romeo and Juliet*, so it was in the context of the Capulets and the Montagues. But, it was a real question, especially in light of the fact that they fight so much. It's like where does this stop? You don't like her. She doesn't like you. You fight and you never really address the problem. It just keeps compounding over and over and over until it becomes this big blowout mob fight, and then you all get suspended or put in jail and it doesn't stop until somebody decides to stop fighting because they don't want to get suspended anymore.

I think that, in light of the world that we live in right now, I wouldn't say completely get rid of security. I do think, however, that we have to make a greater effort to figure out why kids are acting the way they do. Improve student development. We have a student development team in our school. It's run by one of our counselors and she works her butt off, but doesn't have a lot of support. Teachers try to help her, but we can't do a small collective.

We have too many kids. We have so many kids and we can't actually reach everybody. I think we need to have a greater commitment at the school to address these kids and really figure out where all this anger and frustration comes from and show them how to deal with conflict in a healthy way.

We need more community involvement. I wish we had more parent involvement at our school. I don't know if they're intentionally distant or not really present in their child's life, but they need to step up and say, 'This is how you should live' or 'This is how you should handle things.' But, the reality is that some of our parents will come up to school and fight with the kids. They will fight another child who has had a confrontation with their child. You're coming to fight a kid? You're an adult. In those cases, I see where so-and-so gets their attitude from.

Despite all that, kids still need someone who can take some time to come in and dialogue with them. I think that would make a huge difference. They need someone to tell them how the real world works and that teachers aren't just saying this because that's what they have to say.

If we had more parents and more people from the community who actually took some time, it doesn't have to be a lot of time, but actually took some time to come and talk to kids and explain that there's a better way to handle life than the way you are right now, it would make a difference. Our kids don't really have that. They don't have a lot of positive role models in their life. If they could just see someone, I think that would make a big difference.

May 2008

"It gets very militant."
RACHEL BOOKER[15]

Rachel Booker is the mother of two students attending Andrew Johnson High School,[16] a four-year CPS school located in a well-off neighborhood on Chicago's north side. She and her family live just walking distance away from the school. Rachel is co-chair, with Haley Robinson, of Johnson's parent organization focused on curriculum design and implementation.

Months before my interview, her parent group invited me to speak at one of their monthly meetings on the topic of Black and Latinx male student academic engagement. At the time, there was an influx of students of color matriculating into Johnson due to their neighborhood schools shutting down. It was at this talk where I met Rachel, who expressed serious concerns about the school's necessity for policing.

My concern about security here is their training. I don't know if they are trained to de-escalate situations, which worries me because whenever there's a security issue it seems to blow up and the police become involved and it becomes a very big matter. I just think that's related to the training. They are not trained properly to handle teenagers. You know, understanding how to keep the problem from not getting police involved. There was a fair amount of incidents, more than I've been aware of. Every day there seems to be something that goes on with fighting in school.

What's the phrase that I'm looking for? It gets very militant. I think that they [security guards] get too militant and are too quick to bring in police. Instead of trying to make it less of a problem, it becomes more of a problem.

When you think about this school, it's not just about the area. I mean, this is a school that pulls from a number of different communities, which may have gangs. This school is broken up into the International Baccalaureate program, the honors program and college prep.[17] There are neighborhood kids that do a performing arts program. And so, because the school is made up of a number of different groups, you're pulling from a number of different neighborhoods. So, you're not just getting all what you would consider to be 'rich kids.' There are other kids who are involved.

I'm not privy to knowing whether there are gangs involved. I know there are a core group of kids that seem to be continually causing a problem. I heard from a security guard who mentioned that there's like a group of kids that seem to be the troublemakers from closed down schools. If we could get rid of those like 50 or so kids, this school would be so much better.

I found out from one of my son's teachers that there are three kids in his class that are really causing a lot of problems. The teacher has to do everything in his power to control these kids, to get them to just stop acting badly. It's really impeding the progress in the classroom. It sounded like they're pretty bad.

I don't really know where these kids are coming from. And, I don't want to say they're one kind or from one neighborhood because I don't know. The minute these kids came here we [parents] were sort of shut out from knowing who were really causing the problems. I don't know if it's the administration or if it's the security, but they kind of keep things under wraps.

There was an incident that happened. Our parent group got a letter about the incident. There was a mom complaining about a friend's kid who got beat up by security. It was a horrible situation. Something happened, but because she wrote the letter to our group, we became privy to the situation. But normally, we are not privy to what's going on. We had a security guard come to our meeting. We asked him some questions like, 'Who was involved in the situation and how are things at the school?' He was just like, 'The kids are behaving better.' I said, 'Why are they behaving better? What's going on?'

We're supposed to have a representative from administration at every meeting and it's a disaster. I don't think that we realized it until after that security guard was sent as a rep that day. I think that more people see him as the head of security versus the vice principal, who was promoted this year. The guard really came on behalf of the administration. We asked him what was going on and again he was vague.

I mean, the teachers are being accosted. There are incidences fairly regularly, fights in the cafeteria, but it's so muffled. I think it's an administration thing. I think they try to keep things [whispers] under wraps. The only time we find out is when things are written on paper and come to us. If that mom would have never wrote that letter to our committee, I would have never known about that.

The reaction from Johnson's administration is a little disrespectful. I think because security is a very a hot button issue right now, especially in light of what's been happening at other schools, security is a big topic.

There was this issue where a prior student on a CTA bus made threats to current Johnson students. He was saying things along the lines of something's going to happen at eighth period. I believe it was gang-related. So, the students heard this and they started texting each other. I don't know how it got to the principal and the staff, but it got to the police department too. That individual was arrested at 3 o'clock in the morning. He was like 23 years old but he was a prior student here. That kid was arrested. In the meantime, you can imagine what ensued when no one knew he was arrested. There was all this texting frenzy.

That morning, my daughter came up to me and said, 'Do I have to go to school today? There's a threat of violence at school.' I said, 'What are you talking about?' I just thought she was trying to get out of school. Well, it turns out there had been a threat. The school was aware of it. That day security was checking bags, lining up students inside the freshman building, checking all the packages. People were lined up. No one knew what was going on. Half the kids weren't at the school.

Parents weren't sure what to do. I called up the school and asked the secretary if I should be bringing my kids to school. She said, 'Well, there was a threat, but I can't advise you on what to do.' She said to me, 'Stay with your kid and everything will be okay.'

They [the school] should have communicated to parents one way or another. What went wrong? The principal could have text[ed] or called parents. The office should have had information like, 'Someone's been arrested. It's okay. Send your kids to school.' Apparently, they were advised not to tell us what to do, but someone should have.

Our school has metal detectors. When I was here the other day to watch what they were doing, there's a guy that stands sort of in front of the metal detector. He ushers people in. I was trying to figure out what was going on because up on the detector's board there are these lights that light up and sometimes it's green and sometimes it's red.

Now, my neighborhood has a kid at Walter Payton High School.[18] There, when kids go through security, their cell phones will ring, their keys will ring, all these things will ring before they go through security. They have to take everything out and put it into a box like at the airport. I'm very confused because I know that Johnson kids have keys and cell phones and iPods and all that kind of this stuff.

I was looking at our detectors and I was trying to figure out well, why is it sometimes red and why it is sometimes green and why isn't he [the security guard] stopping these students when a red light goes off? He stopped no one. He just kept going like he was herding cattle. 'All right, come on through,' he'd say. He was just doing his job and herding them through. That's for one building. I don't know what goes on in the freshman part.

The school does do random searches. I had heard about a kid where they had found pot. He got stopped and security went to search him and he left the building or rather he ran away. Security ran after him and it turns out that he had pot on him.

I really don't think students, from any school, take security seriously because I don't think that it's being taken seriously here. I mean, we're a school that follows the rules. If we're a standard, then I don't think security is truly abiding by what's going on in CPS. They find weapons here, but they don't want to scare anybody. I hear these things. I don't know where the information is coming from, which just tells me that there is some difficulty in communicating.

We're in the middle of a very rich neighborhood and there's that whole thing where you scare people by saying, 'This is what's going on.' On the other hand, I'm more about knowledge. I think that sharing knowledge is a better way to go about it. The principal thinks there's a thing where you could scare people away and make them nervous.

In addition to police inside the school, we also have bicycle police. They're paid by the alderman's office. I think they're paying for it or at least helping us to pay for those officers. Parents asked for them and they've been here for the last couple of years. They're here at the end of the day, patrolling the area on their bicycles.

Sometimes seeing police to me creates more chaos and more concern, hostility and paranoia. Do you know what I'm saying? On the other hand, if school starts at a particular time, then no one should be walking around the hallways. But, I see that still and I don't get it. Where's security? Who's in charge? Security isn't outside yelling at the kids. They're in here yelling and we see that as militant behavior, but only when something happens inside. I think that's what's concerning.

Stuff happens on the streets. I'm just wondering how they are dealing with the problems that happen inside and if we have enough security to really deal with the problems outside. I still don't know where are the major problems. Where are the hotbeds? Are they in the cafeteria? I don't know. Should there be more supervision?

The community at the school has changed a bit. I know the project kids used to come to this school, but since they tore down the projects, I don't know where those kids are going now. A fair amount of those kids no longer come to this school. But, the community inside the school has changed. Well, I just think it's changed. I guess it's become more Brown, more middle class. I'm not saying more White and more Black. Back then, the school had a much harsher reputation and it now it's getting a softer reputation.

I'm torn with the reputation change. On the one hand, I'm feeling like students need people out there saying, 'Get into the school!' or 'Do this!' There has to be more adults to give direction. Maybe it needs to be the administration. I remember when I was in grade school when that principal came walking out there, it was just like, 'Clear it out [laughs].' She meant authority. People respected her. I see that it's not the same respect with this principal. I don't think that people see her as an authority.

There's one woman that they [students] like. I actually think that there's a tolerance of some security officers here. They get to know the kids and treat them like humans. I see them out there talking and conversing. I think that the security guards have already taken more of a parental role just by actually talking to students more than teachers.

Teachers should be doing both discipline and connecting with students. Today, that role has been shifted. They even ask parents to come and man the doors. Man the doors! Are you kidding me? We're supposed to walk around during key times of the day—lunch and after school for an hour—and just sort of be an extra sort of eyes, just walking around making sure students are doing the right thing. Are you kidding me? The crazy thing is that anyone can walk into this school. The security is really lax. It's not consistent. They talk loud, but that's when they think students are mindlessly walking through the hallways. That's when security gets militant.

Wait. I say, 'militant,' but maybe 'rigid' is the word. I think that when you're in this situation and you're with a kid, instead of saying to the kid 'Hey, what's going on?' If this kid flails his arm and touches someone, it becomes a police issue. It becomes an expulsion. It becomes much greater than maybe it should have been. It's very rigid. I understand it's not acceptable to hit someone. I understand that, but it's just this zero tolerance thing. I mean it's crazy. A kid takes an aspirin and boom. They're taking drugs and they're out.

I think now we rely so heavily on police and guards. There have just been so many problems with school closings. I mean, there's so many of these. I also think ever since the Columbine shooting happened, security has become a much bigger issue than what happened at Virginia Tech.[19]

There has to be some policies in place. I think that kids and adults need to be treated a certain way. I just think that again there's poor communication. Are the security trained to handle what's going on? It's the way security is trained. It's also the way people talk throughout the school. It's how people are communicating. Parents and students need more information.

School policies are on our organization's website. When students walk in, they're supposed to only go in through a certain door. There should be clear and concise rules about the security measures or what occurs. When kids walk in, they only walk through one door. They walk through the detectors. When adults walk in, they have to check in. I mean, someone has to communicate this. Not only should that communication be towards us or on the website, but someone has to communicate it towards the security as far as what their jobs involve.

It's disconcerting what's going on in public schools today. I think it's an issue is for suburban schools, as well the city. Virginia Tech was a private school. Things like that are happening everywhere. Do we create a mass hysteria by becoming overly militant? I don't know.

I do know that schools are a smaller representation of what's going on in the world. I believe that there are certain kids that are treated differently. Whatever's going on in the world, it happens in schools. It's just a reflection. I think that certain kids are treated better based on their level of performance. And, when a kid doesn't act right, instead of dealing with what's behind the act and why they're acting like that, schools and society just automatically kick them out. Kick them out and put them into jail. That's our society.

March 2008

"Good morning. I'm glad you made it."
RONALD HATHAWAY[20]

Over the past three years, Ronald Hathaway has been a "youth service coordinator" for a community agency that networks with one of Chicago's oldest southeast side public high schools. The school is predominantly Black and low-income. He works exclusively with male students on their non-academic barriers and social-emotional learning. Ronald states that his role is to "get them prepared for consistently attending school by putting social services in place that CPS has eliminated over the years."

Some of the supports Ronald provides through his agency include counseling, tutoring and, when absolutely needed, monetary aid. Ronald claims that the youth in his program are a smaller representation of a larger student body that "exist on the fringes of academic success, but also deal with a tough home life." Our interview took place at a Chicago public library near his Bronzeville home.

First off, this school, over the past three years or so, has had a lot of students coming in from closed down schools. This required more security in the form of guards, Chicago police, plus new metal detectors and surveillance cameras. When the kids first walk in, they have to go through metal detectors. They come up the stairs and pass through one of two. There is security guards right there, mostly CPS hired, but a few CPD ones as well. The kids have their bags searched and lay their bags down on a belt for screening just like at the airport. Then, they walk through the metal detectors and get patted down. I see that every day.

The goal is to make sure there's no weapons or drugs getting into the school. I think if they didn't have the metal detectors and it was obvious they weren't going to search kids, they would just walk in right through the front door with all kinds of stuff [he laughs]. But, things still get in. I know marijuana is getting in. I can smell it in the hallway.

A couple of months ago, a kid got through with a gun. One of the police officers, or one of the security guards, saw the kid walking around in the hallway and the kid turned a corner real quick with his jacket pulled back and you could see the gun tucked. They asked him to come back, but he ran off. They actually ended up chasing him about eight blocks and shot him.

Supposedly, the kid turned around and had the gun in his hand and one of the police officers chased him. When the kid turned around and showed the gun, the officer had the right to shoot or that's what they're saying. He got shot twice in the chest. I know he had a collapsed lung, but I haven't heard anything else about it. I would have to imagine that it was probably not the first time he carried a gun into the school. I think kids get guns in quite often.

From what I'm thinking, security is more about appearance. It's the image that CPS is doing something rather than absolutely nothing. One thing about this school is that CPS's entire security division is actually based out of it. Everything that runs through for CPS security comes through my school. They even have their own section of the building. It's amazing that you have CPS security headquarters in the building. A lot of stuff though actually still goes on inside the school.

On the first floor, no kids are walking around. You have the main office and a lot of conference rooms. The second floor is usually contained. Then, you have the third floor, which is where all the mess goes on. Kids walk in the hall, smoke cigarettes and weed. They're just hanging out and nobody says anything to them.

It goes back to appearances. We want to give you the appearance that we're doing things. So, if all your visitors are staying on the first floor, pretty much their entire time they don't see any kids. They don't see the fights and they don't smell the weed. It just gives the appearance that 'Okay, we're actually taking measures.' When you walk in, you see the metal detectors, you see the screeners and the belt, and a couple of officers and security posted up front. It's just the appearance of a safe school.

A lot of security issues happening in the school, I don't have to deal with. Other people have to. I don't have to deal with those things with the group of kids I have now. I've worked with different kids off and on. I've worked in the court system in Indiana as a pre-trial police officer.

I've worked as a residential facility case manager. I actually worked with security in Gary's [Indiana] school system. So, there are a lot of things that I can identify faster than other people can.

I will say that, from my experience, you have to be able to see the signs. You can tell when a kid is calling something [referring to gang signs]. You can tell by the people they hang around, what colors they wear, or if they have a do-rag hanging on one side of their pants. If they're walking or running down the hallway with their crew and you know they're about to do something, you can stop them. If you know the signs, you can get to that kid well before they get in trouble.

The other thing is having a relationship with them. If you've built a relationship, they're going to listen to you. You got to talk to kids. You can't wait until they get dragged into your office. You know, everybody's emotions are elevated, but nothing has to happen. It's just that the work has to happen before an incident. If you can just kind of have conversations with them beforehand, it makes things so much easier in the long run.

With all the beefed up security we've had, I know for a fact the kids don't feel any safer. I had a workshop last year in November with about twenty-five of the kids I work with. We had these notebooks for them to write down their thoughts about school. We were supposed to talk about motivation, but we started talking about things going on inside the school and in different nearby communities. The thing that came up, and what became apparent to me, was that they were all actually afraid to be in the school. So, we started talking about that. I was like, 'How do you guys make it through the day?' Most of them were like, 'Stay to yourself.'

We got all these students from different neighborhoods at the school. You've got kids from 35th [Street], 37th, 39th, Ida B. Wells, the Ickies,[21] and even Stateway.[22] So, they're all mixed up and you don't talk to anybody. You just try to get to your class as fast as you possibly can. You don't want to stand around. You have an idea of where security's always going to be, so you try to stay in that area. There are areas of the building where you don't know if security is going to be there, so you avoid those spots. But, for the most part, a lot of the kids are scared. Even the quote unquote bad kids are scared.

All of this stuff is related to gentrification. Right now, at our school, it's the first time I've really seen its actual effects. They tore down a lot of the housing projects and a lot of the low-income housing to put in mixed-income housing. It's funny because the apartments that are for low-income people I can't even afford. They knocked the price down on some, but I really can't afford those places. They're like two hundred and fifty thousand dollars. That might be cheap in Chicago, but it's not cheap for somebody that came out of the Robert Taylor Homes. So, those people have had to go anywhere in the city that they can.

The issue that they're running into now with the kids is that the city is telling them they have to leave their neighborhood and their school. They have to go wherever the city places them or wherever they can find. Sometimes, they have to move far south and enroll at a school like Julian[23] or Simeon.[24] And, after talking to a few of the kids, they're saying it's actually safer to stay at their old school because the kids from neighborhoods around Julian and Simeon don't know kids from the Robert Taylor Homes and they might have an issue. That's when they become a target for seven or eight hours a day.

Why sit someplace where you're the only person from your old neighborhood and nobody's there to step up for you and defend you? You don't have any power in numbers. It's just not safe to go there. So, if that means traveling across the city and getting to school at 10:30 in the morning and an hour or two late just to be safe, that's what you do. That's what all those kids will do, so they're not a target.

Safety, for the young men I work with, is about having to go through different neighborhoods. You know, Chicago's so territorial. You go three blocks in either direction and you're not around friends anymore. I was trying to do some things with my students this past summer and needed them to come down to one of our offices, which is just eight blocks away from where they live.

The guys were like, 'We can't go over there.' I knew exactly what they meant. I didn't have to go into it. So, imagine having to travel all the way from the west side or south side. There's no telling how many different territories they have to go through. Anything can happen to them at any time.

Something new that's come to my attention is with some of the female students. One girl, I just spoke with, whose family is bouncing around a lot right now, was telling me that she's being approached by men on the train now. She says her friends are too scared of being attacked sexually or threatened and all types of things. So, these kids go through a lot just to get to what's *supposed* to be a safe school for them.

You have to also draw a relationship between gentrification and crossing territories with the growing gang issues and community violence that we've been seeing. It's a big part of the things that are going on now and how the violence rates have been rising. That's one of the things our organization is taking a look at.

You have to look at how people have had to move from different neighborhoods when the housing projects started going down and people from the suburbs decided to move back into the city and buy land, pushing people out. When CHA started to fall, that's when the murders started to rise. You got kids going everywhere and that's a big problem, not just in Chicago but in the south suburbs and even Indiana.

Increasing school and community surveillance has been the city's overall response to this problem because for the most part people believe that security and police are going to be able to fix everything. Over the past couple of weeks, all CPS schools had to go through a security update. At my school, I could still see where it was just the appearance of adding more security while everybody just went through the rhetoric.

Everybody was saying that we needed to increase security, but we really didn't. What they did was pull a security guard off one floor and put him on another or they took a security guard from over here and put him over there. They never actually hired anyone. It was something where they could say, 'Okay, this will calm the citizens down for right now,' but nobody wants to take real action steps before we get to the point of violence.

For there to be real change, it has to be grassroots. We need community conversations and action, money for youth programs, community programs. Parents need to know what's going on now and how things have changed. It's completely different. But Arne Duncan and the mayor know that if they stand at the podium and say, 'Well, there's more security,' then their job is safe for another three months.

For example, I'm trying to get $5,000 for a music program in this school. It's not just like music is the answer, but that's just one of those things I want to put in place for kids so they can have a place to go and have something constructive to do. It amazes me that my school has had so many amazing musicians come out of it, but doesn't have a music program.

It's also just the things that they've taken away. There's so much of a focus on testing now. You know, 'What are our test scores like' and 'what are your students' levels?' You can give a kid a test all day long, but a test is only supposed to find out how well a kid can read or understand math. These kids are struggling with everyday things that have very little to do with academics and there's a frustration because they know they can't perform. They haven't been taught a way to express what their problems are and how to vent them. But, it's going to come out some way. It might not come out in sorrow. It might come out as a fight or worse, a bullet.

Kids see the guy on the street, the dope dealer who's driving the best car on the block. They see the guys that are breaking into houses and everyone knows they're breaking into houses, but too afraid to say anything. Everybody wants a nice life by any means. So, if we're not putting in the measures to make sure kids can do whatever they feel they want to do in life so they can have a good life, a lot of our kids are just going to say, 'You know what? I'm just going to start breaking into houses too.' We've got to start getting away from this testing thing and just go back to the basics. Everything goes back to the basics.

You know, I come from a family of cops, so I don't want to just make a generalization on all cops, but I'm pretty sure that most cops have a their perceptions when they see a group of guys together. If you see a group of guys, chances are you don't care they're over there working on homework, you're going to tell them to move on. They could be sharing thoughts on a book like, *The Autobiography of Malcolm X*. Doesn't matter. Cops will still be like, 'No, you all gotta go.'

If you're a kid in school and you're being yelled at for doing something bad, that affects you. I've seen some security officers, and some teachers, just badger kids constantly. They figure they can fix the attitude of that kid who says, 'Nah, I ain't gotta talk to you.' The negative way security and teachers deal with students, day in and day out, has to completely effect students' day at school. Imagine being yelled at the minute you walk into your school, in some cases, for just for being there.

It's like the young lady that I was telling you about. I just saw her this week and she was having a bad day. She was like, 'I had this one guy following me from three different cars on the train, talking about how good I looked and all this other stuff. Trying to avoid him, I was five minutes late for school and had every the security officer and the assistant principal yelling at me.' She didn't want to be at school that day. Sometimes, I just want to tell the security officers to smile at the kids and say, 'Good morning. Glad you made it.' It could make a huge difference.

When I'm working with my group, it takes you about fifteen minutes for everybody to just calm down. Two weeks ago, I had this kid who was targeted by one of our security guards. This guy likes to really mess with students and he was being especially tough this day. Well, the two got into it and the word is that the guard took the kid into the security office and roughed him up a bit. He comes to me and he's out of it.

While I was calming him down, the rest of my students got amped up. We accomplished nothing I planned for that day. Kids can't process stuff like that. I have to help them do it, teachers have to help them, and that takes away from learning. So, there you have a direct connection between school security and learning.

Actually, I think security guards have replaced teacher-student relationships. When I first started going back into schools in Gary and then in Chicago, it was amazing to me because I remember walking down the halls as a student and if a teacher told me to stop, then I would stop. The presence of a teacher would stop us. I can't say at what point in time kids became more powerful. I just think that teachers have passed their authority onto security.

I see teachers step out in the hallways and say, 'Security, I need you in here.' But, you're an authority figure. The fact that you're a teacher, no matter if you have thirty or forty kids in that room, means you're the authority figure. If you give away your authority to somebody else in the building, then those kids are not going to listen to you. Why should they at that point?

I can't stop teachers from giving up their authority. So, in the last couple of months, I started doing a program with some of the teachers and police officers. It's a b-ball [basketball] tournament. I invited police officers because these kids need to see them in a different way. I understand that I can't say how a cop is going to do his job, but these kids need to understand that we're all human and we need to have some type of relationship-build with one another beyond control. Playing basketball together, or any sport, can help with that and it's getting support from the school's administration.

I know there's this argument that guards should have some form of training in relationship-building before they're stationed at schools. Well, whose job is it really to deal with kids emotionally? Police officers? If you're a police officer or security guard, you're going to say, 'That's not really my job.' And, if your only requirement for the job is a GED or high school diploma, then you're probably going to say, 'You know what? I'm not getting paid enough for all that, so I'm just going to sit down at my post all day.'

Better training isn't going to happen until CPS realizes that it takes more than a high school diploma to be an effective security guard. Not saying that you can't be an effective security guard with just a high school diploma, but it does take a little bit more training to understand how to relate to kids, especially adolescents.

I don't know if you heard about one of CPS's security guards back in November or December who got arrested for stabbing a baby in the eye. She was on the CTA and stabbed two people—a lady and a baby. As it turns out, she was on all types of medication. She was schizophrenic. The day she decided to go off her meds is the day she did the stabbing. So, to my point, CPS needs to understand that security guards are in a very important position. Maybe we need to raise the salary, while requiring certain training.

In the end, it comes down to how CPS looks at schools and pays attention to the lives that are involved. I think that we need to have people who understand how to actually do security. It's about making people feel safe. The guards and officers we have now don't even relate to schools, much less to students, and they're way too reactionary. They need to stop being reactionary to everything. Right now, our security is about making sure there's not a lot of bloodshed when something happens. You know, getting there fast enough so nothing really bad happens and that's all. But that's the least of our time. What about, 'Good morning. I'm glad you made it.'

March 2008

"What are we waiting for?"
TAMEIKA ELDRIDGE[25]

Tameika Eldridge is 17. She is a senior at Robert Latimer High School.[26] Her academic interests focus on American and world history. Tameika has applied to only state universities. "I can't be too far from my family. They're my rock. I need them." Her career goal is to become a lawyer, but she's unsure as to what kind of law she'd like to study. "I'm thinking about criminal justice or family law. Those might be where I'm most needed." As a lawyer, Tameika strongly believes that she can make a difference, serving on behalf of Black people in her community.

For this being a CPS school, I think security is needed and let me tell you why. See, if it wasn't a CPS school, then it wouldn't be as many people as it is. It's overcrowded, overpopulated, more people than there is space. Just bumping into someone can cause a fight and security has to be there. I'm from the block, so I can talk about security inside Latimer and when I step outside, it's also needed. With so many kids moving in from other neighborhoods, I would say from Normal to Halstead on down to State Street, police have to be around—blue lights flashing, roadblocks, and all that.

Some people hate cops, but not all police officers are horrible human beings. Some of them are out there to make sure gangs don't jump all of a sudden on people. If a lame[27] is outside by himself, a gang of boys that call themselves GD or BD[28] will jump on him for the fun of it. So, I'll say that police officers are there to stop them from doing that. Wouldn't you want someone to help you? If a gang of girls come up and jump on someone to the point where they're bleeding, wouldn't you want them to get arrested?

I do see the other side of the issue, though. I think police officers protect sometimes, but other times they do make me feel unsafe. Like, why is there all these security guards standing around the hallways? What are you saying? Must be something bad is going to happen. I have cousins at Chicago State University[29] and I've visited different colleges too. I noticed that I can go around Chicago State all day long, no metal detectors, no nothing, and, nobody stops me, no security. I wonder why I can do that there, and then when I go to my school, it's like hordes of security? It tells me something.

I even sometimes feel offended by all the security at Latimer because everybody in the school knows I'm here for only one thing—my education. I'm not saying that I should get special treatment, but that's all I care about. I don't get in trouble, but they still search you and question you. I wouldn't say they're taking their job too seriously, but it's like all of that isn't necessary. If you have to do all of that, then there must be a problem. Something people aren't talking about or looking at.

When you walk in, my school checks your bag, makes you strip down, and wait in line for 20 minutes while everyone else is being searched, even in the worst weather. If you're class starts at 8, you have to get to school at 7:30 because there's going to be a line of 30 kids already standing there. This is all because they [security] are afraid some kids are going to bring gang life into the school. The neighborhood is full of gangs, but all this security is not getting at the root of the problem.

This is a neighborhood school. I think a school is like a family and you need to take care of your family members. You also need to understand that your community is your extended family. If you're ignoring poor people, then your community will continue to get poor. Then, of course, you're going to get poor kids coming into your schools and a poor environment within your school because they're dealing with a poor environment outside. Your school is not going to prosper if your neighborhood doesn't prosper. There's a connection between the two. For your school to be well and good, your neighborhood has to be well and good.

Until people see the connection between school and community, security will be seen as necessary. Schools will choose cameras over books simply because they don't believe that it can get any better. Teachers believe that the kids will tear up the books and they aren't there to learn from the books, so why buy them? We need to help the community first.

I was raised where I had people I could go to and talk to. I have all these people around me that care about me, so I feel like that's why I'm succeeding and on a successful path. All these other kids, I know they're not getting what I'm getting. I feel like they're not getting support so they act out. No one is asking them what's going on at home or why are you coming to school and your clothes aren't clean or did you eat last night? These are basic things that a lot of kids aren't getting. They end up coming to school mad about different situations and taking it out on other people because no one is paying attention to their home life, nor are they paying attention to their school life.

We have school counselors, but how are you going to have only two counselors for all the kids here? There's no way they can pay attention to each individual child and be able to see what's wrong. You know, progress can't come until you look at everybody individually. You can't look at everybody and just write them up for whatever reason just because it's the same on the surface.

You got all these kids from these rough neighborhoods and they probably don't have parents that support them. I've been attending academic programs all my life, but at the same time I have a mom who cares, neighbors who care. We might not be the richest, but they still care about me and a lot of kids don't have that. Like this boy today was on his phone. He was like, 'Man, stop calling me!' I was like, 'Who's that? Was that one of your girls?' He's like, 'No, it's my mom.' A lot of people don't have good relationships with their parents. They don't get love from home or people in their community. Then, they come to school and got security guards lined up here and here and there.

See, that's the thing. I think at every school there are some good teachers and counselors, but the system is still really frustrating. When you been in it for so long and you're getting nowhere because nobody is working on your side, you want to drop out. I feel our principal isn't working on our side. The whole system and all of that is not working on our side. It gets frustrating and eventually kids feel it, then they explode. I believe if you bring in good teachers, counselors, and social workers, you also need to make sure they're dedicated and will treat students right.

Some of the most inspirational people I know are educators like my auntie—she's a vice principal. She was saying how teachers have to play three roles. They got to be our teachers, sometimes our parents, and then they got to be the counselor or the social worker to help you through your problems. A dedicated counselor or social worker can help you, which takes pressure off of the teacher. It will eliminate some of the stress on her. Then, she can do her craft and get into her job and be more inspirational—not just to one or two kids, but to half the class or the whole class she's teaching.

People always want to throw money at this situation, but I really think more so than the money is the family situation. It plays a really big role. Let's say we're all poor, but we have parents who are dedicated. Me and my mom have never been rich, never. We've always been, I guess, lower class. But, she takes me to school every day, works with me, gets me a tutor. Money doesn't matter much because we value education. Whether you're poor or rich, if you value education, it's going to work out. But, see everyone is not like that because they don't know. If your family's not there or your parents are on drugs or no one on the block gives a damn, then it plays a huge role in how you see education and life.

I say stop waiting on the government to help. At a certain point, you have to take responsibility for yourself. I've walked into several other universities, even other high schools, and they've been better than my school. They don't have graffiti all on the wall when you go into the bathroom. And, I've never once said, 'Wow, this place is better. Since we don't have this, I'm not going to school or doing my homework.' It's like I know if these people have the best, but I can have it too. That's why I'm bettering myself to get out of this situation.

I'm not waiting for the principal, or the alderman, or the mayor to lift my community. I'm going to get my education and give back myself. It's winter now. Waiting on them is like waiting on summer. I can't wait. We can't wait. So much time has been wasted and still no changes. What are we waiting for?

February 2008

YEAR 2008:

QUESTIONS, REFLECTIONS & RESOURCES

Questions/Reflections

What exactly is the role of police and security guards within public schools? We acknowledge on a surface level that their presence is for the safety and protection of educational environments. Yet, testimonies from this 2008 section question that premise. Officer Johnson, for example, sees police as more symbolic, wondering if her presence and that of her colleagues is actually needed. Haley Robinson believes that school policing creates more of an "incarceration-type situation" with little rhyme or reason as to its existence beyond perceived fear of violence or curtailment of drug sell and use.

One of the more critical statements posed by participants in this segment comes from Jocelyn Rawls: "I think police in our schools and neighborhoods is abnormal." She identifies omnipresent security as peculiar because of what she has observed at other academic (predominantly White) institutions, where police are not openly used to surveil and punish bodies of any particular ethnic group. Indeed, Jocelyn sees her school security measures as more of a "Band-Aid" failing to heal personal and communal wounds—most notably mental health issues.

What must also be highlighted, when it comes to ultra-securitized, majority-minority urban schools is the treatment of students. The racial inequalities they face, in and outside of their learning centers, are reproduced in two essential ways: one, through institutional practices and two, through cultural representations of racial difference. With respect to the latter, males of color, for example, are stereotyped as aggressive, unintelligent and salacious. In terms of institutional practices, racist sanctions against minority youth produce feelings of despair and failure, pushing many to permanently exit schools as soon as they are legally permitted to leave.

Educational professionals in 2020 and beyond must realize that much of the connective tissue in how we interact with Students of Color is part of societal beliefs grounded in implicit and explicit bias. Undeniably, cultural misconceptions guide the hand of judgment, objectifying Black and Latinx peoples to the property and instrument of White supremacy. Silenced and excluded youth feel and live through societal demonization, and often react in the most perfunctory of ways in order to maintain their self-worth—ranging anywhere from defying educational goals and teacher authority, to hallway violence and disruption, to fighting others, destroying school and community property or dropping out of school altogether.

Without question, educators must take time to reflect on their own racial and class biases of minority youth and to dispel whatever longtime myths they internalize. Doing so will not only help improve classroom teaching and experiences for all learners, but also afford teachers a wider lens to appreciate the overall fullness of Students of Color—their talents, gifts, assets, ideas and beliefs. By taking this time, schools can build stronger academic, cultural, social and emotional connections with minority youth, as opposed to hastily shrinking and disempowering them through regulation, suspension and exclusion.

While the above approach by no means directly confounds the larger system of White supremacy, it can however function to help engender more ethical learning spaces where youth can give voice to their issues and develop best practices alongside teachers and staff. It also holds potential for transforming district- and state-wide educational policies to actually address the needs and concerns of school and community participants.

Below are several resources that I strongly encourage readers to consider and examine in pushing their thinking and practices forward in their problem-posing and problem-solving work with minority students, families, and communities.

Books/Articles

ALEXANDER, M. (2010). *The new Jim Crow: Mass incarceration in the age of colorblindness.* New York, NY: The New Press.

CAMMAROTA, J. (2004). The gendered and racialized pathways of Latina and Latino youth: Different struggles, different resistances in the urban context. *Anthropology & Education Quarterly, 35*(1), 53–75.

Davis, A. J. (Ed.). (2017). Policing the black man: Arrest, prosecution and imprisonment. New York, NY: Vintage Books.

FORMAN, J. (2017). *Locking up our own: Crime and punishment in Black America.* New York, NY: Farrar, Straus and Giroux.

KENDI, I. X. (2019). *How to be an antiracist.* New York, NY: One World.

MCCAHILL, M., & FINN, R. L. (2014). *Surveillance, capital and resistance: Theorizing the surveillance subject.* London, England: Routledge.

MITCHELL S. D. (2014). Zero tolerance policies: Criminalizing childhood and disenfranchising the next generation of citizens. *Washington University Law Review, 92*(2), 272–319.

NANCE, J. P. (2014). School surveillance and the Fourth Amendment. *Wisconsin Law Review, 79*, 80–137.

NOLAN, K. (2011). *Police in the hallways: Discipline in an urban high school.* Minneapolis, MN: University of Minnesota Press.

ROTHSTEIN, R. (2017). *The color of law: A forgotten history of how our government segregated America.* New York, NY; London, England: Liveright Publishing.

Organizational Websites/Other Resources

The American Civil Liberties Union (*www.aclu.org*) is a national nonprofit, nonpartisan organization that focuses on civil protections under the law. It defends the rights of people and groups on such issues as racial justice, voting rights, LGBTQ rights, women's rights, national security and free speech.

The Advancement Project (*www.advancementproject.org*) is a multiracial, multigenerational national organization whose vision and goals are aimed at struggles for human rights, equality and justice in an inclusive democracy that is devoid of racism.

The Southern Poverty Law Center (*www.splcenter.org*) is a US nonprofit organization focused on monitoring the activities of hate groups, teaching tolerance, and engaging in legal disputes around such issues as voting rights, immigrant justice, criminal justice reform and children's rights.

The Urban Institute (*www.urban.org*) is a nonprofit research organization that researches policies and practices and generates solutions and strategies that address present-day issues and concerns.

YEAR 2008 NOTES

[1] A pseudonym.

[2] A pseudonym.

[3] Hyde Park Academy High School, once titled Hyde Park High School and Hyde Park Career Academy, first opened its doors in 1863. It is a public four-year high school located in the Woodlawn neighborhood on Chicago's south side. In 2012, Hyde Park became the fourth Chicago public high school to become an International Baccalaureate (IB) school. The total minority enrollment is 100%, and 98% of students are economically disadvantaged.

[4] Altgeld Gardens was built in 1945 and named in honor of Illinois politician John Peter Altgeld. It is located on a 157-acre site on Chicago's far south side, near 130th and Ellis, in the Riverdale Community/ Lake Calumet Region. While there has been a commitment by the city to preserve and reuse of many of the housing units in the past, a number of buildings have been demolished with more facing potential demolition. The housing project is a 99% minority public housing community hosting 8,000 community members, 90% of whom are Black and 63% of whom are living below the poverty line.

[5] Rockwell Gardens was located in the East Garfield Park neighborhood on the near west side of Chicago. Constructed in 1958, it was the first public housing development in the U.S. to be funded by both state and federal dollars. Rockwell was given the last name "Gardens" due to the

vast, award winning flower beds that lined its perimeter. Predominantly minority and low-income residents filled its 1,126 units until 2006 when Rockwell was eventually demolished.

[6] The Henry Horner projects, also called the Henry Horner Homes, were named after the first Jewish governor of Illinois, Henry Horner, who served from 1933 to 1940. The CHA public housing project was located in the near west side community. The projects were constructed between 1957 and 1963 and contained seven, 7-story buildings and four, 16-story high-rise buildings all with 920 units. Residents were majority-minority and low-income. Henry Horner demolition began in 1995 with the last building razed in 2008.

[7] A pseudonym.

[8] Chicago Alternative Policing Strategy (CAPS) is a community-driven policing strategy designed for the Chicago Police Department to bring police, local government agencies and communities together to prioritize problems and prevention efforts in Chicago neighborhoods. CAPS was launched in 1993 as a pilot program in five of the city's 25 police districts as a means for dealing with community and police divisions documented as beginning in the Civil Rights Movement.

[9] A pseudonym.

[10] A pseudonym.

[11] Northeastern Illinois University (NEIU) is a public university in Chicago, Illinois. It is located in the community area of North Park

with three additional campuses in the metropolitan area, serving approximately 9,000 students in the area.

[12] Blue Light Cameras, also known as Police Observation Devices or PODs, have been used in U.S. cities over the last decade or so. Connected to street lamp posts, this surveillance camera system was designed to be utilized in urban areas with the hardest hitting crime as a method for limiting or discouraging criminal activity. In 2004, Chicago police and municipal court systems used captured images/ video from PODs to present evidence in criminal cases, particularly those involving gang activity, narcotic operations, reverse stings and police safety.

[13] A pseudonym.

[14] A pseudonym.

[15] A pseudonym.

[16] A pseudonym.

[17] The International Baccalaureate program offers college-level courses and the opportunity to earn college credit. Founded in 1968, the IB Foundation, originally called the International Baccalaureate Organization (IBO), is headquartered in Geneva, Switzerland. It provides various educational programming for youth preschool through high school. It is considered the highest tier of educational programming.

Honors Program courses, at the second tier, generally refer to exclusive, higher-level classes that proceed at a faster pace and cover more material than regular classes. Honors classes are usually reserved for talented high school students who excel in certain subjects.

At the third tier are College Prep courses. They are a set of core high school classes—e.g., English, math, science and social studies—that are meant to increase curriculum rigor and college readiness beyond remedial coursework.

[18] Walter Payton College Preparatory High School is a four-year selective enrollment magnet high school, which draws academically eligible students from various parts of the city. Unveiled in 2000, Payton Prep is named after National Football League (NFL) legend Walter Payton, a former member of the Chicago Bears who died before the school opened. The school is ranked one of the top schools in the state in areas of math, reading, science and writing.

[19] Virginia Polytechnic Institute and State University, known as Virginia Tech, is located in Blacksburg, Virginia. On April 16, 2007, Seung-Hui Cho, an undergraduate student at the university and a U.S. resident of South Korean origin, shot and killed 32 people and wounded 17 others with two semi-automatic pistols before killing himself. At the time it was the largest mass shooting in contemporary American history perpetrated by a single gunman.

[20] A pseudonym.

[21] Harold L. Ickes Homes was a Chicago Housing Authority (CHA) public housing project in the near south neighborhood on the city's south side. Built between 1954 and 1955, these projects were named

after U.S. administrator and politician, Harold LeClair Ickes and were part of the State Street Corridor, which included other CHA properties like the Robert Taylor Homes, Dearborn Homes and Hilliard Homes. The Ickes consisted of eleven 9-story high-rise buildings with a total of 738 apartments. In 2011, the final building was demolished.

[22] Stateway Gardens was a Chicago Housing Authority (CHA) public housing project located in the Bronzeville neighborhood of the south side of Chicago. Stretching alongside the Dan Ryan Expressway, adjacent to the former Robert Taylor Homes, Stateway Gardens construction began in 1955 and these projects were named after the street they were built on. Stateway was a cluster of eight high-rise buildings with approximately 1,644 apartments. All of the property was demolished by 2007.

[23] Julian High School is one of nine CPS four-year high schools serving the far south side in the Washington Heights neighborhood. It was opened in 1975 and named after Percy Lavon Julian, a Black research chemist. The high school is majority Black with 97% from low-income households.

[24] Named after Neal Ferdinand Simeon, a Black educator and school administrator, Simeon Career Academy is a public four-year vocational high school located in the Chatham area on the city's south side. The high school opened in 1949. Application for admission to the school is required for all students who are interested in attending. Simeon has a college-preparatory and career-focused curriculum focused in different fields such as Accounting, Architecture, Auto Tech, Barbering,

Carpentry, Cosmetology, Computers Culinary Arts, Web Design and Welding.

[25] A pseudonym.

[26] A pseudonym.

[27] A colloquialism used amongst youth at the time of this research to describe someone who lacks social skills, is unoriginal, nerdy or not with the times.

[28] Gangster Disciple (GD) is largely a Black gang formed on the south side of Chicago. The GD's formation goes back to the 1960s with its acknowledged founder Larry Hoover. In Chicago, GDs have a long and hostile rivalry with the Black Disciples (BD), which was founded in 1958 in the city's Englewood community by David Barksdale, Richard Strong, Dirk Acklin and Prince Old Timer. Both organizations have a strong legacy in the city and are revered by gang and non-gang members alike, with purported memberships totaling about 40,000 respectively.

[29] Chicago State University (CSU) is a public university located on the city's far south side. It was founded in 1867 as the Cook County Normal School. Originally launched as a teachers college, CSU offers degrees in areas of study such as Business, Pharmacy, the Health Sciences and Education.

YEAR 2009

"It's like the chicken and the egg."
CHRIS HARRIS[1]

Chris Harris has been a CPS high school teacher for nearly a decade. He has taught the last five years on the city's west side at Dolores Huerta High School—a four-story, cube-shaped structure that almost resembles an office building or hospital. Demographically, the school is roughly 50-50 Black and Latinx. Chris teaches freshman through senior students in such courses as Contemporary American History, World History, World Studies and Modern United Nations.

Given his suburban upbringing, Chris finds city schools socially and politically challenging. Despite being a White male working in a majority-minority school system, he believes that CPS is where he's most needed: "These kids need me. I might not look like them, but I have the kind of compassion that's beyond race."

At the time of our interview, Chris was the Chicago Teacher's Union representative for Huerta. He says that he took on the role out of a desire to "generate change and equity" at his school. For Chris, Huerta sorely needed a union rep that "put parents and kids first." We met in his classroom during his 30-minute prep period.

As far as security goes, I think we actually do a pretty amazing job here at Huerta. I used to teach at Andrew Johnson High School[3] on the north side, so I've seen a very lax security with no X-ray machines. We had metal detector archways installed, but were never used. At Huerta, they are strictly enforced. Students know that they have to go through them and, for the most part, I think everyone feels confident that there are very few weapons in the school.

Right before I got to Johnson, there was a rumor a year or two before that the principal had brought in police and dogs to search for guns and drugs and they found quite a bit. It was mostly on the White students and the more advanced AP and IB students. The parents turned around and initiated a lawsuit. They sued for improper search and seizure because apparently they had female cops searching male students and male cops searching female students.

So, the parents filed a class action lawsuit and won. They received a check from the district and then, from that point, the school stopped doing any sort of searches like that. They'd have the metal detectors, but not all students would have to walk through them. The detectors would go off, but no one would actually search your physical body.

Now, at a school like Andrew Johnson, you wouldn't typically think about search and seizures being carried out, much less finding weapons on advanced White students. I guess the expectation obviously was that the more advanced students were probably less likely to have anything like that and so they were probably searched less frequently.

Yet, students from Cabrini-Green and the more impoverished areas that fed into Andrew Johnson probably were subjected to more searches, so I guess they would be less likely to bring something in because they knew they were going to get searched. When a full-on search actually happened, I think those students that normally don't get searched and feel like they can have anything on them without getting caught were finally caught. It stood out because obviously it was Andrew Johnson's reputation—mostly White, rich and upstanding.

Since Johnson has an open campus, students probably feel they can do whatever they want. At Huerta, it's a closed campus. Once they're in the building, they're pretty much stuck here. If you leave the building, they don't let you back in, which cuts down on what's able to get into the school. Johnson has more neighborhood options of where students can go, but also the expectation that they're not going to be involved in violence and all those things. Plus, parents don't want their kids to be completely stuck in the school. Actually, I think the building's layout limits that. Their cafeteria can't handle all of the students. So, there's no physical way that they could keep all of them in for all those periods without a drastic change to their lunch schedule.

At Huerta, we have four different cafeterias that we can easily put students in. But, there's also the expectation of students bringing things in that's not at Johnson. The odd thing is that I think this school is perceived as much more dangerous than what it probably is. There's the assumption that drugs are rampant and that everyone here is involved in a gang. I recently asked my students about this and they estimated about 60% of the population was involved in gangs, which seems incredibly high. Though, I've heard our administrators say that it's down to around 10%.

I asked my students if there was any way that we could survey and find out what the actual numbers are on gangs, drug use and stuff like that. I think it would be good for them to know so that we have an expectation of what Huerta is and a real understanding of what it's like because I feel we're just working off assumptions. If gangs aren't much of an issue, then why are we putting all this energy into police and security guards?

Even though administration says the gang population is down [to] 10%, the students here have to wear uniforms. The uniforms for me are partially about image perception. Do they want students to feel more professional? I don't know. I think [gang] colors were a big deal back in the day, but now there are so many ways gangs can signal with their symbols and stuff. Are the uniforms really necessary?

As a teacher, administration very rarely informs us on what the real status of gangs are here at the school. Last I heard there are probably eight or nine different active gangs at the school. In the small section of the school that I teach in, I probably have a few students involved in gangs. I would say that a lot of students active in that are in other parts of the school. So, it's not obvious to me.

I've asked some students if they were in a gang, but that's like one of those questions you should carefully avoid, you know? I would say that, if a student wants you to know, it's because either they trust you or they're trying to intimidate you or something. They'll let you know, but generally I find those students that are really involved actually are very cautious about it and very serious. They don't joke about it. I mean, it's a business for them. So, I don't set out to ask every student. I don't ever touch the students and never search their bags either. That's something we have the deans and security staff for and the police.

Given all the issues around the school, I think security has a purpose here. It's like the chicken and the egg. One, I think students actually prefer it because it makes them feel secure. At the same time, I think, if you respond with too much force, then you're going to get an equal amount of resistance. I don't know. I guess it's one of those things you'd like to be able to experiment with it and say, 'What if we became a little bit more relaxed and gave kids more trust and responsibility?' But, if anything ever happened to them, we'd ultimately be held responsible.

We should definitely explore opportunities of opening up the campus a little bit more for our students. But, at the same time, I don't think students are ready for that. We've done simple things like non- or out-of-uniform days and those have always gone well. A lot of students have pretty much respected it and responded well without abusing it too much. They do realize that it's a privilege and so they respect that. I think it would be nice if we continue to do more of that.

Huerta's come a long, long way from where it was four years ago. Students were pulling fire alarms, so they could go outside. Since we have all these different floors, they could find the person they wanted to fight or talk to by pulling the fire alarm. Once they went outside, they did whatever they wanted. And then, they were coming back into the school without having to go through metal detectors. They've changed that now. When we do have to evacuate the building, everyone has to file back through the metal detectors again. It's great because that was sort of like this big question mark. Without being screened again, what's the rest of the day going to be like?

We used to have huge fights in the streets. A lot of it was precipitated by poor policies like when Austin High School[4] closed down. CPS started shipping about 20–30% of Austin's population to us, which were mostly African American students. This definitely conflicted with the politics and the gang issues of Huerta because it was mainly a Latino population.

This was known as a Latin school, but in reality it's now about 35% Puerto Rican, 30% African American and 30% Mexican. So, you know, you can't just say that's it's a Hispanic school anymore. You have three different groups, all different gangs, competing for control of this school. I think CPS decided there's a way that they can establish some boundaries and live together. But it took a full year to get to that point. Imagine a whole school year with students fighting over any- and everything. The space to them became smaller because they were at odds with others over racial and cultural issues.

Daley's Renaissance 2010 is ridiculous. People at the board tend to be late career individuals and have probably been out of touch with competing communities. I can't tell you the last time those people at the board have probably been to the Austin community and know what's going on at the grassroots level.

This school didn't find out that Austin students were coming here until like a week or two before school started. Students just started showing up. There was really no time to plan anything. No one from the board said, 'Hey, this is what's going to be happening. You're going to have some problems, so Huerta, anticipate it.' I just don't think CPS's vision was big enough. They were just focusing on Huerta without knowing what was going on in Austin and what was coming into this school.

That year we had the highest number of violent incident reports in the city of Chicago. But, we promoted it as being a good thing. We were going to document this. We were going to take care of these students and push them to be accountable for things. I asked my students the other day, 'How many of them look forward to sending their own children to Huerta?' I was really shocked. I had about four or five students in each class who were really adamant about sending their own children here. They wanted to send their kids to Huerta because this is their community school. This is part of their heritage. They have high expectations that Huerta is going to get better.

Other students are kind of aware that Huerta may or may not be here. The building will be here. The school will be here. Whether it's called Huerta or not, or it has some other structure to it, is their bigger question. All of these other charter schools are opening up and getting a lot more support and funding than we are. With the innovation that's going on in those schools, public schools are getting less and less. There's still huge political pressure to keep Huerta here by the community, but I think it's a self-fulfilling prophecy.

If you keep draining us and narrowing down our programs and what we offer, it makes us less competitive. So, if you're looking at reasons why students should come to Huerta, we've gone from seven or eight small schools down to four. We're even narrowing down what we offer at the school. While we are increasing our test scores, our population is decreasing. We're in a community that's gentrifying and this building has the kind of physical layout that is very well-suited for small schools or charter schools to be brought in here.

If you're looking to revamp an entire community, bring in new families and big businesses, you know, establish a whole new culture, then Renaissance 2010 works just fine for you. But, if your school is closing down, you can't afford where you live, where you eat, and you're being pushed out and moved around, and policed all while doing that then, guess what? That's a poor policy, it's an unfair policy. We know that here. We're just trying to protect the students from what we can, at least while they're in the building.

With CPS's lack of community understanding came more police and security guards. With that, I think, came negative effects on student learning. Teenagers, and just people in general, always want to rebel as you exert more control. They're going to resist. I'd rather have a student rebelling about wearing an earring in class or not coming in with a uniform because I think that can prevent the larger things down the road like having a totally out of control class.

I do know when there is a fight in the school that's what the students are concerned about. If there's a fight going on kids are gonna run to whichever floor it's happening because they want to know if it's anyone they know that's involved. Those days are always sort of a lost day because students are just out there. I think security definitely impacts their ability to think freely.

Beasley Elementary[5] was built with a brick wall facing the Robert Taylor Homes, which is no longer there. The wall was physically set there to prevent any sort of gunfire from hitting the students. Those students were told they have to walk two square floor tiles away from the wall in a single line. That's how they led them through the school with absolutely no talking and they achieved that. I think that's an example of negatively impacting one's ability to think a little freely and more abstractly. Beasley was at the point of impacting kids and their learning.

It seems like security has become this panacea. Security is sort of what you do after the fact, you know? I think there needs to be more of an emphasis on teaching students what's the proper way to behave here and what to expect. Our students are taught, and they'll even tell you, when you see a crime happen in your community, don't report it. Just focus on yourself.

The problem is that when you focus on yourself, you're not concerned about activism and protests. You're not out there self-policing your community. You're just worried about what you as an individual is doing. You're not holding other people accountable to another standard. Even students that witness a drug deal in the class don't say anything about it. That's a real issue.

I acknowledge why students don't step out of their safety zone. It just seems like it doesn't matter how much security you have in the classroom. If people are operating with the understanding that they can get away with anything they want and no one's ever going to report them unless it's an adult or security, then how do you address that? The response is security, which, for me, ends up taking away from opportunities to think freely and to learn.

November 2009

"Kids are going to be kids, no matter what you do."
EDUARDO HERNANDEZ[6]

Eduardo Hernandez is a dean of students at Dolores Huerta High School.[7] He has been in charge of security and discipline throughout the

building over the past five years,. Though Eduardo operates with a high
level of autonomy, he is still under the general supervision of Huerta's
principal as per CPS policy.[8]

Eduardo doesn't see himself as solely a disciplinarian. He strives to
incorporate "positive behavior support systems and intervention strategies
as much as possible" into his work with students and staff. His office is on
the school's third floor. Inside are two filing cabinets and a huge metal desk
cluttered with papers with six walkie-talkies standing at his arm's reach.
Eduardo's bachelor's and master's degrees hang from the wall together with
two pictures of his family.

In my office, we handle more of the higher code violations. We
have six code violations that we follow according to CPS's Code of
Conduct.[9] It's one through six. There is a dean on each floor, and I also
oversee those deans. I also oversee the security guards and together we
handle most of the major code violations.

The security measures we have here [at Huerta] outside of guards
roaming the hallways are cameras on each floor, metal detectors when
you walk in and X-ray scanning machines. There are also Chicago
police in the building. We have been able to communicate really well
with the police in the community, where we have it set up for them to
meet us outside at dismissal time. When it's time to be released, they're
posted at different corners of the neighborhood.

Security is necessary because the school is made up of two smaller
schools and sometimes they don't get along. We have the Achievement
Academy, which is on the third floor. These students are students
[who] have not graduated from eighth grade, but are too old to be

in an eighth grade setting. So it's a transitional program for them. There are about two to three hundred students in that program. Then, there's the general school, which is the freshman curriculum through the senior curriculum. That has about seventeen hundred. So in total you're probably looking [at] about close to 2,000 students.

In our first period beginning the day, teachers are already here. Students are coming in. Unfortunately, our culture, our specific culture, has a lot of students that come in tardy. So, throughout the first period, it gets very difficult to try to simply just settle in. We're having to put the students inside the classroom or get them away from the locker because they've missed 20 minutes of their education. We try to get them into a classroom regardless whether they have their jacket or not. If they need their stuff from their locker, maybe a book that they need or something like that, we try to assist as quickly as we can.

So, the first part of the day, that very first period, is more settling in and identifying any major problems that we might have throughout the day. For example, when they [students] are coming in, you might come across a student that tries to bring in a weapon or tries to bring in drugs or tries to bring in something like that. We're spending that first part of the day just handling those situations immediately.

Every student has their bag searched or scanned. Security's been trained to identify what can potentially be something. If they feel that there is something that needs to be looked at, in most cases, they'll look inside of the bag and usually find what it is that they've seen on the scanning machines. Finding something usually happens on a weekly or daily basis. Lately, it's happened a little bit more than usual. And, there are so many factors that can determine why it's happening.

One, it could be where, you know, kids are now settled into the school or school year, so they're feeling more comfortable where they're trying to see what they can do and get away with. I think another thing is that usually right around January by the third quarter, we have students that are being released from juvenile or from the Department of Corrections (DOC). These are basically repeat offenders and they have some form of history. Unfortunately, these kids have maybe created some enemies here or in the neighborhood.

The DOC kids come out and word gets around pretty quick that a certain person is out and another student is going to retaliate or something like that while in the school. I think recently we just had a week where we probably had about six or seven incidents like that. We, as disciplinarians, anticipate what part of the season it seems like we're going to get the most trouble, whether it be winter break or a spring break [pauses to respond to security personnel on walkie-talkie].

Traditionally, Huerta's always been known to be a school that has had some form of issues. Even when I was growing up, being part of an urban school, you always heard about so many things happening at Huerta. Now, whether they were happening or not, I don't know. But you constantly heard about something going on, even if something wasn't happening. I think that because of people's perception and because of what they're saying about the school's image—that it's not a good school. It's not just because of the neighborhood. You can have a good school in a bad neighborhood.

School shutdowns definitely don't help us, though. It has meant more security here. The first year that I got here, we did have some major issues with new students coming in. I think that the new students probably felt like they needed to come in ready because at any point something might happen. So, that wrong perception might have had them coming in a little bit rougher.

A lot of students weren't happy that they had to travel through maybe four or five different neighborhoods to get to this particular school. If you're part of a gang and you have to cross four rivals to get here, then you're already coming into the school with this rush and that's not going to help anyone.

I'm a firm believer that urban kids are urban kids. Whether you're on the north side, west side, east side, or south side, if you're living in Chicago, to me, you're pretty much the same all the way across. Some staff might have pigeonholed kids right away, but I didn't see it that way. I simply saw it as these are urban kids. What's happening now is that you've got more kids coming in from different neighborhoods and different cultures. So with the mixture, the blend of gangs, all of a sudden things get broader.

You always have your security according to your numbers, depending on your enrollment. With the Achievement Academy setting itself in place, which wasn't something that was here before, and the school closings obviously brought in more students and more problems, we had to organize our security based on ratio per student.

I think that paying attention to our security-student ratio has increased trust with the staff. I think we've taken all steps necessary to ensure safety in the school, whether it be beefing up our police officers outside or posting security on the floor in twos or threes. And, in some cases, identifying where the major spots are and trying to hit those places. I think that organizing the structure of the school, in terms of where the disciplinarian should be and where the administrators should be, has also helped.

In the past, administrators were all in the main office. The dean of students was in the office, as well. They put my office on the third floor because it's in the middle of the school and we can kind of watch floors both up and down and see what's going on in the hallways and stairwells. They've used empty classrooms to place an administrator on each floor. So now, you have an administrator on each floor, deans of students on each floor and me in the middle of the building. So, small measures like that have probably gained more confidence in us trying to control the behavior of the students.

I do feel that our students feel safe to a certain point. I've come to realize, probably in the last year or two, that most of the school's incidents stem off of what happens in the neighborhood. I feel that there are a lot of students that are not doing what they should be doing academically and have some very, very poor judgment. They make very bad decisions and they do things that are just outright dumb sometimes. But for whatever reason, they seem to come to school still and I feel like they find school to be their safe haven.

As crazy as it sounds, there are just some kids that you wonder why are they here? I feel it's because it's their safe haven. I really do, even though they're bringing in things that are unsafe. I won't be the first one to close my eyes and be shocked about it.

We also have to look at the urban community and understand that there are factors out there affecting these students, affecting families. A student's justification to why they should make money, even though it's wrong. So whether it be, God forbid, stealing an iPod or anything for a quick buck, they have to do it. I've got students that come for lunch, simply just to eat, maybe because they don't have the opportunity to eat at home. For all we know, maybe this is their best meal. So realistically, the school is a safe haven for them.

Now, when things stem off the block, maybe a situation from Saturday or Sunday, you're coming to school Monday and you're a little edgy. There are so many factors, but I think a lot of it has to do with what's happening out there. Schools closing and people having to fight for crumbs is real. It's real for us because we have to deal with the violence that comes from it.

The number of security we have to deal with students is okay. I think we're leveled off at a good number where we can kind of contain all the issues that we have. What I don't like is probably our lack of training when it comes to security. We're talking in general because I can direct a security guard on what to do according to our school policy, but I think there's still some foundational training that security should already have that they're not getting, whether it be certified through the state, through CPS, or whatever it is. I'm not really sure. I can't really identify that.

If I have a security guard, for example, [who] was in the military, then he has a foundation. I mean, one of the first things that they teach you in the military is you stay at your post. Okay, so he's always at his post. I think that's because of his training. Unfortunately, that's not the case with every security guard here. For some of them, I feel that maybe it's just a job. I really can't say. [Responds to security personnel on walkie-talkie.]

Security is sometimes defined very lightly. I see it as making sure that you're ensuring the safety of all children, all staff, securing the building, and identifying and preventing any issues. I don't think we've been trained in some areas for those particular things and that might be a big risk or big liability. We tend to skip over those things. For example, at the airport you're screened very well because of terrorism. Sometimes, I wonder does something really major need to happen in order for that same sense of urgency to be increased in schools.

I think that the sense of urgency should already be there only because we're an urban school. We're in the middle of a neighborhood with a big blend of students from different communities and different gangs across Chicago and they all have different issues. We should maintain a sense of urgency from 6:30 in the morning until 4 in the afternoon. It's not one of those grand old types of missions. It's about saying, 'Hey, we have a job to do.' We've got to make sure that every student comes in safe and that every student leaves safe at all costs. That's all across the board, whether it be Huerta, Andrew Johnson, or Lane Tech. Security in any position, especially in an urban setting where you have these issues, needs to be that way.

I don't hire or train the guards. That runs through the administrator, which is the principal of the school. He is the only one that actually does the hiring of the security guards. I don't train them because that's not the position I'm in. I'm a disciplinarian. I'm not certified to train security. I spend most of my day speaking to the guards [picking up one of his walkie-talkies] and giving them directions.

I do know there is training for them throughout the school year with professional development days. But, they're trained in a very broad spectrum. It's not like taking your five security guards and you to identify specific things in your school. It's a little different when you have a general assembly and you're trying to perform training. I don't think it has the same effect. Some of our guards are verbally abrasive towards students. That's definitely due to a lack of training or a lack of foundation. I think you have to be trained to identify your market.

We're dealing with urban kids, so our guards need to keep that in mind. If you're dealing with urban kids they are, for the most part, a very defensive group to begin with. This means they feel they always have to be in defense mode. If your approach is to be abrasive, you're probably gonna get a negative response from the child. You have to be able to communicate with these students, understand them.

One of the things I've learned over time is that once a teenager identifies that they cannot have any trust in you, you've lost that student. It's very difficult to regain their trust. This isn't an adult now. This is a child that's still going through growing pains. So, if you cannot communicate with an urban student in their setting, you're probably going to get some real bad responses from them.

It doesn't mean not to be stern. You might have to take somebody down because of some type of physical action or something like that. But, I think for the most part we can prevent a lot of the issues if we simply identify kids and their issues and see if we can work within those issues. We don't want to be everyone else giving them low to no expectations. We can't promote the same culture that the urban city has already given to these students. They're already expected not to succeed.

If you bring them into a setting where they feel this is their safe haven, where they can probably get some form of peace or maybe not get shot today inside the school, then we have to learn how to actually react, how to respond to these kids. These are kids. Kids are going to be kids, no matter what you do. You have to be able to connect with them, speak with them, but be stern with them. There is discipline, but it has to be done the right way. It has to be done with protocol. It has to be done correctly.

Some guards defy me because they feel they know students better than I do or what's best in a situation. That happens quite a lot. When it happens, my guards get a warning basically saying, 'Hey, if you'd handle it this way, you would get a better result.' The better results aren't usually what they're expecting because they're frustrated and confrontational. But, they need to know that you could have done this when approaching the student the right way. That's all it took.

Another thing too is that, again we're a community school. That means that we're tied to the community in some way. So, you have an employee, a guard, who's not dealing with a student according to the Code of Conduct. They want a pass because that's their cousin's or an aunt's nephew or something to that effect. Guards can't do that. It's a liability and it's unacceptable.

As for our security detail and parents, we don't get a feeling from them that they think security is too much here. Now, I might come across parents that'll try to question the discipline process or why we're doing something in a particular way. That's common at any school. On the other hand, I think parents are satisfied with the fact that we're taking every precautionary measure for students to be safe, whether it be a metal detector or police outside.

On the whole, we've gotten some good responses from parents on security because we're a community school. They know how things are on the block. Even our local school council is very much involved because they know many of the students and their parents. It's like a big family and a lot of it stays within the family. So, I don't get a lot of bad responses to what I'm doing as a disciplinarian.

I do hear parents say, and I agree, that we need more counseling over suspensions and expulsions. Huerta needs to develop that. There should be more relevant programs to meet the needs of our children. We have students that are in special education classes that are receiving services for their behavior. But, are they receiving the right services? Are they in the right programs? Are they being taught by teachers that are certified to teach in that particular field? I think it's an issue.

I also think that, for the most part, many of our kids aren't placed correctly in order to succeed. What I mean by 'placed correctly' is you can be in a classroom, but are you receiving the correct curriculum? Are you receiving the correct attention? Is the person that is with you trained and certified to deal with your particular learning style?

Our community-based programs have to be more relevant to what goes on in the community and not necessarily create something that is done simply by a book or something that just meets their goals. You can get a program with state funding and work with a hundred kids. But, are you working with kids that need the help with those issues that are going on in an urban school or are we just taking a hundred kids because we need that number to get funded for the following year? I don't know. Where's the impact?

I just don't think our students are being serviced correctly. What are we doing? Do we have the right programs in place? Do we have the right teachers in place? Is the administration doing what they're supposed to be doing? Our school has come a long way. We've done very well in the last two years. We've identified many of the key issues that are important. I think that's probably my biggest concern.

From the parents that I speak to, I don't know if we have enough relevant programs or enough relevant teachers or staff that can identify the real issues of these kids. It's not necessarily because it's a disobedient child. There might be a core issue that is causing their behavior. Security guards can't address that. Their job is to ensure the safety of students, that things are in order. In terms of identifying the issues of students that's where you hope the deans, the disciplinarian, the administration, counselors, social workers and psychologists step in.

If we don't get beyond schools as prisons for these students, they'll continue to see it as normal. The metal detectors are not something that's out of the norm for them. Being searched is not out of the norm. Going outside and seeing police officers are not out of the norm. Now, if I had a kid that's coming from the suburbs or somewhere in Alabama or Beverly Hills or some rural state that's just *not* Chicago, then I might say, 'Let's sit down and talk.' But, you just don't come across that.

Most students I come across see security as is normal. You don't find them questioning it. You find them coming in, taking off their shoes and jacket, taking off their bags, putting it through the machine, and moving along as if everything's normal. We have to change that, so that it becomes abnormal to them and then they'll question it like the student from Beverly Hills.

School security is a lesson for these students. It's something that I think they just fall in line with. While it may teach them a certain form of control, it also teaches them that you have to be someone who is responsible, someone who has integrity, and someone who makes ethical decisions. That's fine, but it also teaches them a certain behavioral pattern that is acceptable in society for a young man or young woman of color in the urban city. In the end, they'll see doing what security says as correct, as functional, and lessening their chances of failing out there in this urban society. I'm not sure if that should be the core lesson.

November 2009

"Don't disrupt the educational process."
ISABELLE ESPERANZA[10]

Isabelle Esperanza has been a public school educator for 15 years. The past four years she has been teaching Latin American Studies at Huerta High

School.[11] Given the school and community's history of violence, security methods and technologies for curtailing both have become quite visible to her. "In all the time I've been teaching, the policing of schools has become incredibly normal." Despite this, she states that her time in CPS has given her a tough veneer for handling student conflicts without involving SROs or police. According to Isabelle, students around the school know her as a strict but fair teacher.

The most obvious security measures here at Huerta are definitely the guards, especially when you first walk in. We have metal detectors that work all day, every day for students and anyone else, except for maybe faculty or staff. We have between 15 and 18 security officers. I don't think our security is for the amount of students, but more because of the way the building is built. It's the many levels.

There's one security officer on every floor, sometimes two. We have four in the lunchrooms and on the athletic side of the building. So, I think it's because of the structure of the building, not that there are so many students. We also have two police officers which is the norm for certain high schools that the board (CPS) assigns. They're stationed here every day.

We also have deans. Technically, it's one dean per floor. I think it's kind of strange how it's done here because I've been to other high schools and they have a dean of curriculum or a dean of discipline or a dean for staff or an assistant principal for those areas. But here, there's like a dean for each floor and then some. That's like four, five, six and seven deans. Again, I think it has to do with the building's structure.

I do see why we need deans, but it's not the traditional use of a dean. Here, a dean is like, oh my God, a security guard or police officer.

Two or three years ago our population was larger and the gang tensions, the rivalry, the turf battles were bigger. It was terrible. It was so clear when we knew things were going to go down. So, we definitely needed security. But, we don't need them now. They can be better used elsewhere and better trained. I think that certain security guards, the way they come down on students, is not the best way. I think they have to be retrained in the things that are their purpose so that they don't make problems worse. I was a dean for two years and some deans can make matters worse. It happens with everyone. The teacher can escalate a situation or defuse it. It depends on your approach.

We've lost a lot of students to charter schools and whatever, but I was thinking the other day if we really need the amount of security that we have. I don't know if it's necessary given the numbers. I think we need to be more effective. They have to be strategically placed throughout the day and there are times when you have to decide what to do and pick your battles. Let some things go and pick on the things that are more important like fights in the building.

I've seen students around here taking their time to get to class and security goes ballistic on them. Sometimes students just tune them out. It could go both ways, though. Sometimes you try to understand the role of a security officer, the responsibility in getting the students to class. I don't know if students are affected. Some kids just tune them out and don't care and they know they can get away with taking their time. Whereas other kids are really trying to get to class, but just need more time and they get yelled at.

I honestly think that's about retraining. You know, some kids can bring the worst out of you because they show no urgency. They stroll in late, aggravate the class, and they disrupt the lesson, if it's already started. Then, if you question them, well, 'I just came from my locker' or 'I'm coming from this or I'm coming from that floor.' But, they've been told that they only have four minutes, no matter where they're coming from. Students should show more urgency and guards or deans should show more restraint, depending on the situation.

For me, security guards don't really have a direct impact on what I do as a teacher. I'm already up front in the class and doing what I'm supposed to do, so I don't need them. I just do what I have to do. I'm not going to make guards a big issue in affecting my class. Students know what I expect and what I'm going to put up with, so I don't have many discipline problems to request the presence of a security guard to take a student out.

Occasionally, yes. I will have some student who crosses the line or maybe that day I'm fed up and I'm not going to put up with him. So, I'll call security. But, when they come, some of them just walk right in the middle of a lesson. They need to be a little more courteous. When you come to the door say, 'Excuse me. Is so and so here?' Don't just barge in and bring drama to my classroom. I'm strict when I'm teaching and I try not to distract the students.

It bothers me when the educational process is interrupted. It bothers me that security is walking through the hallway giving a heads-up to the kids and their walkie-talkies are so loud. That's how they disrupt my classroom, they're walking around and that thing is at max. I mean really. Are you that deaf? Every time they walk by, it disrupts my class. That's what I'm talking about. That has to be retrained. I shouldn't have to tell them. They should be sensitive to certain things.

I think it's a priority in schools to have the least amount of disruptions. Don't disrupt the educational process. I don't need you to add to the many other things I've got going on. So, please no more drama. Plus, I don't think students fear them anyway. They know what they can get away with and what security guards can and cannot do to them. Students know they don't know their names and they probably don't care about knowing their names either.

The guards are just not as effective as we want them to be. It's about effective training. Also, some of the comments they make to kids are inappropriate. I'm talking about security guards *and* deans. Some of them get too friendly. This is not a buddy thing. You're not here to make friends. You have to be seen as an authority. If you exercise that, you're going to be respected in the measure that you conduct yourself.

You can't play with kids today and then tomorrow try to show some authority. That's not to say that you don't understand them, that you don't care for them, that you don't love them, give them a pat on the back, but it's a fine line. I think a lot of that comes from proper training. They have to understand how to deal with kids.

We have to have high expectations for these kids and the security guards have to understand that we just can't say, 'Oh well, this is an inner-city school, so what do you expect?' Well, you listen, I expect you to take it seriously as you would if you were working in a suburban school. Why would you discard that? These kids deserve the same as those in Winnetka or whatever school.

Maybe if we held higher expectations for all our kids, we wouldn't need security in the first place. We wouldn't expect anything else from them [students] but their best selves. Maybe we could rethink our need for all this security, but I don't know how to go about that. Even if I were to say let's try no guards, certain CPS policies are already in place for that not to happen. We can try next year to take away the metal detectors and see what happens. It might be a good idea.

On the other hand though, I've heard of maybe one student, back in the day, who brought a gun in. We don't even know if it was loaded. I did witness one who brought in a Swiss Army knife, but she forgot to remove it from her bag wherever she was the night before or something like that. Drugs are an issue, but these cameras don't pick up drugs. So maybe it would be a good project to see. Even if you have undercover guards, you know, just to see if students would even notice.

I *do* think that students need to know that we have high expectations for them. I've talked to my students. We talk about topics like expectations and a lot of them say that they're aware that we don't trust them. Some of them believe that we don't have high expectations for them. But, that should not be the case. We need them to know that we expect their best. Security guards have to truly believe that too. We need to model high expectations in order to see a change in behavior and I think that our students will rise to the occasion.

The problem with all this school security began, in my opinion, with the mayor's Renaissance 2010. When CPS phased out several high schools in 2003 and forced students to walk across gang lines to get to school, so much changed. Yeah, the Board [of Education] really doomed us with that one. I wasn't at Huerta during that transition, but I heard that just when the school was doing better, they transferred in all these kids. They didn't want to come, but they did, crossing gang turf, taking one or two buses, and the school couldn't provide transportation for them.

Some students couldn't transfer because they didn't have money for bus fare. Also, because they knew the dangers they'd encounter coming early in the morning or leaving here late at night because of the gangbangers. It was some serious stuff. It impacted school safety and even enrollment here because some kids opted to go to other schools like charters.

When I came to Huerta, the violence had already started. When I came, the transfer students were already here and weren't adjusting well. It was rough because they were constantly being pressured to participate in a gang or being actively recruited. It was rough I tell you, going down the hallway and this one kid is hissing. Hissing is a gang sign for the Cobras. So, either he's a Cobra or he's calling you out as a Cobra and you have to respond.

Gang colors were a problem too. It was a mess but everybody was alerted to it. Some of our security guards who had been here for a long time were like informants. They knew the gang signs, the colors, the looks and the hissing. They picked up on things quick. They know when something was going to go down sixth period and it's going to be on that floor or it's going to be outside at dismissal.

Some kids would get texts about what was going to happen and tell me or the security guards. That was a rough period, but it's over now. We see the light at the end of the tunnel and we're in transition to move on to better and greater things. There is less violence in the school and, in my experience now, very little gang-related things. It's mostly petty stuff between girls about guys and why two students don't get along. They're not getting along because of something that happened over the weekend and it comes into the school because the issue was never resolved.

My students are always talking about having more counselors instead of guards. I know guards can be reactionary, but it's hard for me to imagine schools without police these days. It just sounds so romantic. How are you going to implement it [no security] on a daily basis with violence still interfering with the educational process? I really don't know. I think systems are in place for a reason. Guards are here to protect and teachers are here to teach. It's a concerted effort. It just can't be all about security, though, like I've seen. Teachers have to feel that we're supported by security guards and security guards have to feel that we support them. There needs to be a balance in this kind of work.

Administrators also have to be an effective, not just lip service. You could have security, but with more trust. You have to start with trust. I think it's a whole combination. Students have to understand that they don't make it easy for us. They really don't. And, security guards and teachers should reevaluate themselves and their roles in schools. How can we treat our students better, raise our expectations, and be fair to each other.

We talk about security guards watching students. Well let me tell you, students are watching them too. They're watching everything and learning from us [adults]. It's a kind of curriculum. It's the things we teach students sometimes without actually saying it. For one, I think it's like what I said about security guards needing more training when working with kids. They can't send them mixed messages. It only confuses them about authority.

And two, it teaches some kids that the guards are here to protect them and teaches others that the guards are here to discipline them or lock them up, but that's at any school. You see the confusion? As a teacher, my job is for you not to be confused, but security and all they bring disrupts what I'm trying so hard to do. We have to have balance.

November 2009

**"If you're not doing anything shady, you have
nothing to worry about."**
JOSEPH MARTÌNEZ[12]

Joseph Martinez is 18. He's a senior at Huerta High School.[13] He has been there since his freshman year and is a resident of the local community. Joseph lives with his mother, uncle and two younger sisters. After graduating, he plans to go to college and major in criminal justice. "I like Huerta and my neighborhood, but I can't wait to get out. I really need to spread my wings."

School uniforms are mandatory at Huerta. We wear at them because of the gang situation that's going on. The colors some kids wear is against another gang or whatever. The gangs have certain colors, so if they see somebody wearing a certain color, for example blue, they might mess with them. So, the school makes it a point to have us wear uniforms.

I do feel safer with a dress code, though. Other schools, like Lane Tech, don't have a uniform code but they're gangs all over that school. We have to wear uniforms because we're probably like just a regular public school and Lane Tech is a college prep school. They get the choice of not wearing uniforms, but we have to wear them so we don't have to deal with problems such as gang activity.

All the security here is because of what happened in the past, so they're making it a point to make sure nobody has a weapon or anything illegal they could bring into the building. We have cameras right in the middle of the hallways. Some people say some work, some don't. I think they see it as an advantage to do something if the cameras don't work. You know, let's do this and do that. Let's run the halls or whatever. Me, myself, I've seen the camera room, so they actually do work. I don't mind them at all because I ain't doing nothing wrong.

I'm actually writing a research paper about school security. If we put more cameras in schools and communities, I'd back it up a 110% because I don't want nothing going wrong in my neighborhood. Although some may think of it as an invasion of privacy, it's better to keep the community and school safe, you know? Some crime committers might not care. They just have that thinking. They don't care that there's a camera. They'll still shoot or whatever, but at least they can identify the actual person that did it and not the person that didn't.

Personally, I don't think more security is a bad thing. I just think every student should have the mind state of no distractions, no matter who's in the building. The President could be standing there, but you just continue doing what you're doing and don't be nervous or nothing. If you're not doing anything shady, you have nothing to worry about.

When I first came to Huerta in my freshman year, it was bad. It was, I have to say, the worst year. For me being a freshman and seeing everything going on, I'm telling myself, 'What'd I get myself into?' But since I'm a baseball player and I wanted to come here to play baseball, I didn't let it bother me, as long as I kept away from trouble and did what I had to do. I felt like I didn't have to worry about anything.

I think the message security here tried to bring to us, and still do, is why come to school have to worry about getting into trouble or getting into altercations. We're in school to learn. If you're coming to school to disobey the rules, then just stay home or go somewhere else, you know? Everybody else is trying to learn and move on to bigger and higher dreams. They have and goals that they want to pursue.

I always hear students talk about less security or even getting rid of metal detectors. I don't know about that. I don't know if there's anything that could replace metal detectors or any other machine or technology that can catch somebody having something on them. I think metal detectors are great. I don't think there's any other machine that can do that. I believe that everything is fine the way it is now.

I'm not trying to throw my community or neighborhood out there like that, but I wouldn't be able to trust anybody coming into this school because they might have a weapon or something, you know?

That's why I think it's important to have these technologies to see if we're going to be safe or not. We need that.

What's another strategy to security? I don't know. Maybe one day people won't have to fight or kill each other over petty things. Maybe one day everyone will have an opportunity to get where they want to be in life. Until then, security guards and technologies are needed to make sure no one is hurt or killed. How can anyone be against that?

November 2009

"School is still school and they're still teenagers."
LAWRENCE KITTLE[14]

Lawrence Kittle has served a combined 11 years as a CPS teacher and administrator. He is in his third year as principal of Huerta High School[15] on Chicago's west side. Historically, the school has served nearly 100% Mexican and Puerto Rican working-class students. School closures under Ren 2010 changed those demographics considerably.

In 2005, Huerta received a large influx of students from shutdown schools. Staff and faculty believe expedited enrollments of Black youth into Huerta created a cultural rift that intensified aggression between students, particularly amongst Black and Latinx gangs. With the school's already long record of violence being further extended, parents felt compelled to seek out other educational choices, which gradually diminished Huerta's student population.

At the time of Lawrence's tenure, the school's student composition, according to CPS's website, was 70% Latinx (Mexican and Puerto Rican),

26% Black, 4% other, with a majority being middle- to low-income. He admits that his promotion was initially met with some opposition from parents/staff, who argued that he had limited classroom experience. Lawrence feels that it was more about him being a Black man. With respect to the former, Lawrence represented a growing trend in Illinois education, where untenured teachers were attaining a Type 75[16] certificate to become principals.

As an urban, public school we deal with security issues in and outside of the building. Since I've been here the last three years, we still have issues. However, there has been an increasing calm over the last year. My first year, we had a lot of issues coming in from the community. We're in a major urban area, a major 'hot spot.' Students entering and exiting the building are really high points of our day because of all the traffic that is moving in and around our building. When I say traffic, I mean we have two major thoroughfares outside where anything can happen.

I think what has made been our school safer is the care, the planning, and resources that we have for when our students enter and exit the building. The type of staff we have, the security guards that we have, the deans that we have, the teachers that we have, the administration and, in addition to that, the students. Although students are sometimes connected to the issues of people having conflict, a higher percentage of kids, 70–80%, do not like to be involved in conflict and run away from it. There is a smaller percentage that gravitates to conflict and sometimes that exaggerates what's going on.

Our resources such as security guards, metal detectors, come with a budget. When I first came here, we got CPS-funded security and then we used some discretionary funds to actually hire more guards. And, that's what we chose to do because of we are one of the largest high schools in the city. We had close to 2,600 students. Enrollment has declined over a few years and now we have roughly around 2,200, which is still a large student population.

Enrollment is down for a few reasons. Charter schools are growing and Mayor [Richard M.] Daley has Renaissance 2010 moving forward. He wants to create another 100 schools within the system, part of them charter and part of them public. In this community, we probably have at least five–seven new charters and parents have a right to advocate for their sons and daughters. They want to put their child in a different school, hoping it will be better.

In addition to charters, this area is growing and developing. Gentrification is going on, so people can't afford to live here, therefore they move and new people who can afford the area come in. It's made for quite a shift in what we do here. But, I think those combinations has our school enrollment declining.

Huerta is completely one school, no small schools or schools within a school. We are, however, a school of what we call, 'smaller learning communities.' This is something started several years ago. With the Department of Education being a resource for funding it, the teachers and the culture of the school decided to give each school community a theme, if you will. It is still one school, one principal, one budget, but divided into different academic communities.

We have journalism, communication, law, math, science technology and a military academy. We had a performing arts and world language department, but that has been combined into what we call, 'The International Studies Academy.' We're also one of the few schools that have what we call an 'Achievement Academy,' which houses students who did not graduate from eighth grade, but too old to be in elementary environments. They have a different curriculum, a different unit number, their own budget, but there's still one principal in the building—me.

Earlier this year, we had a police shooting that occurred and the LSC got involved. It was related to all the student traffic outside. A police officer was shot. There were some students involved and they were about maybe a block or half a block away from the school. It was about five–seven students and I think one of them was shooting and a police officer in the school responded.

The officer went down the block and was accidentally hit with one of the bullets that were fired. It was someone who didn't go to this school, lived in another community on the south side. You know, those are the challenges that we have. I think every urban city school has that issue at dismissal time or at entering. People come around those schools because that's where students are and they are attracted to that because they're either trying to solicit a deal or pick up on young girls.

Like I said, I hired more security guards for the inside of the building because I thought there wasn't enough. I mean, we're a large building. I also strategically moved many of my deans, who were on the second floor, to every level. I felt it was important to have a dean on each floor and have at least two security guards on every floor. When our kids eat lunch, somebody has to be in the lunchroom and somebody has to be monitoring the floors. This way we're able to handle several issues as they happen and, trust me, they happen every day.

With the added security, I think students and staff feel safer. I do. I think they appreciate it. A lot of the time I tell the teachers there are more students than us, but there are more teachers than there are administrators, so their involvement in monitoring the floors helps twofold. They know the kids and have a better relationship with them because they are in front of them every day. They can also demand that the kids be respectful to each other, be respectful to the adults, and then monitor when that doesn't happen. Whenever an issue comes up, we have administrators, deans and security guards on those floors that can assist.

Chicago and other cities are experiencing gentrification. In Chicago, Daley and Arne Duncan[17] are closing underperforming schools. They have a history of it and it makes sense to not allow that to happen. When you do that, you have to send students somewhere to get their education. Sometimes that requires kids to cross certain neighborhood lines that they usually don't do. But, at the same time, condoning poor performing schools is almost turning the cheek, saying there's nothing that we can do. These neighborhoods are going to stay this way if we don't do anything.

When schools close doors and students have to cross those lines to get free education, they have every right to, but you need help to set some things in place. I think for the most part CPS has tried to do this. They've allocated some resources and funds so that when those kids come to school, they feel supported. We have people here from different communities who know the community and help students who cross those lines by sort of transitioning them into a new building that's not familiar to them.

When I first came to Huerta gang issues and race issues was an issue. We had some of the same kids in gangs, same race, having conflict with each other. The Latinos were fighting against each other and the African American kids were fighting against each other in different gangs. The perception is that it's racial. It wasn't like that. Once we saw that, I tried to find out the issues, sitting students across the table from each other and mediating. You know, 'What's going on? What is this all about?' A lot of times it was cliques and people looking the wrong way at each other. I tried to get them to see each other as human beings. That was half the battle.

Having people who can sit down and talk and try to build relationships is one of the reasons why a lot of the fighting was curtailed. We dialogued a lot. We sat and talked with kids. We were on the corners at dismissal because that presence was very important. Not saying that it stopped them from fighting [he laughs] because there were times when I was out there with other deans, and students still fought.

After a while, students matured but, fortunately or unfortunately, we had to make some examples out of some of them. If you aren't coming here to learn and we've given you opportunities to rethink what you're trying to achieve, then maybe Huerta isn't for you. So, there have been some dismissals of Latino, as well as Black kids.

Having a safe school environment is about having structures in place first and foremost. You need to identify who your students are. Identifying a time frame for when they enter the building and a process for coming in and how they should come in, having a dress code and making sure every student has an ID. In the city, security checks are the norm. I grew up in the suburbs. We never had to have that. We were bussed. We walked into the building and went about our business.

Today, you have to take into consideration that gentrification is mixing urban people together. Urban schools are closing and students are being mixed too. So, you have to monitor what's coming through your doors when kids walk in. If they have metal, you check. Sometimes, you have to randomly do things because they do bring in knives and Mace and other things that could be used as weapons, which are not permissible. Sometimes, they're not trying to harm anybody. Some people are using it just to protect themselves getting to the bus station or home at night.

Students may be involved in other activities, but it's zero tolerance for that in schools. You can't bring any of that in. Every CPS school has a zero tolerance policy for bringing in anything that could be used as a weapon. So, we put those structures in place and make sure we abide by those rules. The kids know it. We communicate it to the parents and let them know the ramifications if their child is caught doing that.

Once the kids come in, we have a process for getting them to class on time, which is a huge issue for us. If a kid is not in a classroom and they're lurking around the building, then the odds are that they're to do something, whether they're ditching class or looking for another student or looking for another student to make out with. It's going to be something, which is why we have digital cameras. We've evolved. We have about 120 cameras in our building, but we still don't cover all of the areas that need to be covered.

We have several doors, but we can't chain the doors. They are locked from the outside coming in. But you can't stop the kids from leaving if they want to leave. Sometimes, kids open the doors for their friends who leave to go get something to eat for lunch or try to bring something in and our cameras monitor that. We communicate the schedules, what period is what, when kids are eating lunch, and where kids eat lunch.

They [students] have their IDs to identify when they have their lunch periods. We have their class schedules on there, their pictures on there, names and so forth. So there are a lot of things we have in place. We're trying to make sure we identify who and what kids are ours and where they should be. The staff has all this information too.

In addition to security personnel, every CPS school usually has two officers who are scheduled to be in the building. Here, we also hire off-duty police officers, so they can deal and manage situations when they arise. I believe in doing that. They're on call, so when things happen like when students cross the line or maybe when parents come to visit and cross the line. Yes, sometimes parents cross the line.

Parents can get irate just like students. They mainly get irate about the treatment of their child. Sometimes, students cross the line when they get into verbal conflict that may get physical with a teacher. Sometimes, students get physical with each other, which is usually the norm whether it's boys or girls or a combination of both. We always have those challenges and mostly they're verbal. But every now and then, they do get physical. And we follow what we call the School Code of Conduct for the Chicago Public School System,[18] which used to be called the Uniform Discipline Code. So, that has evolved and it's evolving as we deal with issues within schools.

As I mentioned before, sitting down with various gang-affiliated students and having dialogue is something we do regularly or in certain situations. We also do something called peer jury, where our deans refer students who may have committed a violation. Instead of being suspended, they go in front of their peers and talk about what decisions or choices they could have made for different results.

We also have parent conferences but, before that, we really try to sit students down or teachers down, and talk about what the issues are, so people can feel like they're being heard. If there's a disagreement, what is it about? If you feel like you were disrespected, what was it about? People get an opportunity to be heard. They may not get the end decision in their favor, but at least they can't say they didn't get heard.

If we can't get resolution there and teachers need to meet with a parent, we bring parents in. We sit parents and teachers across the table from students so they can hear them talk about what their issues are. Usually, both sides are at fault in some degree. But, sometimes it's important to have parents hear how their child has disrespected or is being disrespected. Some of their issues range from very petty stuff, to boy and girl issues, to what kind of clothes you wear, what you do after school, where you do it at, and all this other kind of stuff. It's like a soap opera and they bring that into the school.

In the end, I definitely think the conferences are effective because what we're doing is actually teaching our young ladies and gentleman how to resolve issues without getting physical. Many times they don't have those skills, so they need to get it somehow. Sometimes the parents don't have those skills either [he chuckles].

Sometimes, we have to stop conferences because the parents don't get it. They want to be the loudest. They want to use the most profanity and we have to let parents know that if we can't be civil, then we're not going to go any further. We've had to cancel some meetings, but sometimes parents are able to make adjustments and sort of get through it.

Overall, the typical response to school violence has been to bring in more cops. This is understandable in some cases, but other things can suffer like the mental health of our young people. In my eleven years of school experience, there are alternatives that can be used to bring a fullness of balance to school environments.

If I reflect on my high school years, we didn't have metal detectors. I'm quite sure we had security guards, but you didn't see police officers on every corner or on the floor as you were walking down the hallway. Maybe a culture shift or a cultural change has to occur where students and teachers feel they're able to walk through their own hallways and doors without fear of being accosted by someone because of what you're wearing, what you look like, or just because you're different.

We need to start early with our kids, giving them different kinds of experiences where they can understand that being a bully or an aggressive person can go both ways. 'Do unto others what you would have them do unto you.' I say start early, getting our kids involved with having different types of experiences. Sometimes getting them out of their communities, getting them out of their homes, having several different kinds of camps over the summer can help.

I saw this program on TV today talking about camps where kids have resources and activities so they're not dropping out. You know, giving them different types of experiences where they value their education more than they value, not necessarily friendships, but the temporary relationships that they have when they're going through high school.

I think that if kids got more connected to things that happen outside of school, then a lot of the aggressive behavior that ends up being either verbally violent or physically violent, would be looked upon as something very silly, immature and doesn't need to be given that much attention.

In many of our urban areas whenever a school is highlighted for violence usually there's more to it than just the behavior of the kids. It's probably an element of the community that comes in. But, schools are exploited and highlighted because of what happens inside them, *not* what's hitting them economically or socially. I would say 80–90% of our student body is doing what they need to do and love coming to school. Besides, many of the deviant things that teenagers do are ordinary. School is still school and they're still teenagers.

It's exposure. I think that adults and communities need to be able to put different things on the table. Expose these kids to something, so that they are not making the choices they are making because some of them are easily influenced. Going after the bling-bling[19] or the fast money that usually either can get them hurt or shot or mixed up in the wrong crowd. We can put different things together for them, but we just need the resources to make this happen.

November 2009

"They might just tweak."
LISSETTE LÒPEZ[20]

Lissette Lopez is 17 and set to graduate from Huerta High School.[21] She transferred into the school in her junior year after her neighborhood school shut down, due to low student enrollments and test scores. She travels by bus and train across the city to get to school. "It takes a lot to get here. There's nothing closer that my mom feels comfortable with, so I take a train and a bus." Lissette's plans after high school are to attend a state university and major in criminal justice.

Every day, students go through metal detectors and are patted down by police. If you forget your school ID, oh brother, forget about it. You are *not* getting into school. I left my ID at home once, and that was all I needed to remember to keep bringing it. Going all the way back to the south side and then back here again is not cool.

Students have to wear uniforms too. It wasn't like that at my old school, but here I definitely get it. There's a lot happening with students and gangs and violence. Our uniforms actually make me feel safer. I know students like to wear different colors and all that, but it can cause problems, especially at Huerta. The school closings changed so much for me and others. That's why I'm here.

I knew some people at my old school that came here and I wish they didn't. I wish the mayor or the city or whoever made a better plan for all this because it's been too much for me. That's why I thank God for security. There's a lot of student fights here. Teachers think the fights are just outside, but I see people getting punked[22] in the hallway and bullied in the bathroom.

The metal detectors we have kind of make me feel more secure, but then again I really don't know. Like, maybe you might have something in your book or you're wearing something and the detector doesn't beep. Girls wear stuff in their hair that could be used as a weapon, like needles or a little pin, and the detector might not beep. I still think the detectors are needed to make us at least feel safer.

I know some schools don't use them [metal detectors]. They think there's no weapons around or whatever. I still feel like if you're going to have metal detectors in one school, they should have them in all because anything could happen in any school, not just one school. All of them should be working and everyone has to walk through them, even teachers. You never know if a teacher is in a bad mood that day. They might just tweak.[23]

Besides metal detectors, we also have [security] cameras. I think cameras help reduce crime in schools and communities. I've seen on TV how they [police] sometimes see criminals on the cameras they use.

But, then at the same time, I wonder if they really use them because where I live, it doesn't seem that way. I live next to a corner store, so there's a whole bunch of little gangbangers or whatever right there every time. I don't feel safe because I don't think the street cameras see them. It's like two blocks away and they're just standing there. I don't feel safe walking because you never know if somebody's going to come through and do a drive-by.

I think more security would make a big difference because it prevents things from happening. If we have security and police protecting our community, then someone isn't going to get away with something all day and I don't have to worry about nothing in and out of school. Inside, students could get into an argument and things might not happen because of the security. So, they might wait until after school to get into a fight. But, if we have police outside with a lot of the staff and deans and security guards, they can prevent a fight or whatever from happening.

When I came to Huerta, things were bad here. I was like, 'I'm scared.' I was scared of things happening every day. But, security was letting students know that they're watching us, that they cared about our state of being because they're there to watch out, make sure nothing happens. It was a little different than what I was used to at my old school. But, once I got here, I was like, 'Oh yeah, bring on the security.'

Now, I'm okay with security I see here. We might even need a little more [giggles], but I think it's okay with how things are right now. You know, if you can't trust people coming into your school or your neighborhood, then you need security. Doesn't that make sense? Trust

is so important. If you don't have it and you're scared of other people,
you might have to call the police. Don't you agree?

We could make things so that everything's less about security and
more about where I trust and care about you. But, would that really
work? I don't think so because people my age, they'll stab you in the
back, literally. They'll gain your trust, but then later on, they're going
to be trying to hurt you or something. We need security here and when
I graduate, I bet they'll still need it.

November 2009

"We're treating the symptom rather than the cause of the disease."
MARY TAYLOR[24]

*Mary Taylor is a guidance counselor at Dolores Huerta High School.[25] In
her 10 years at Huerta, she has seen many changes in student behavior,
mostly as it relates to technology—cell phones and the Internet. A large
number of students in Mary's caseload come to see her after being kicked
out of class, usually for conflicts with a teacher or another student. She
states texting, coupled with bullying, is an emerging problem at the school.
Her students choose to handle their issues through, as she puts it, "nebulous
cyberspace" rather than openly reporting peer pressure to an authority figure.
"Even though I recommend that students speak to a dean or a teacher, they
often refuse any adult intervention for fear of being seen as a punk."*

At this school, students have to pass through metal detectors when
they enter. There are X-ray machines like at the airport. If a student

sets it off, they may be wanded. Then, there are security guards on each floor and security over in the gym. We could certainly have ten security guards on every floor, every minute of every day, and things would still happen because we're not getting at the root cause. We're treating the symptom rather than the cause of the disease.

Teenagers love to try and play around with the rules. They still find ways to get stuff into the school. They wrap up drugs or weapons in a lot of material and get it through. They know that if somebody wants to get somebody, they're going to find a way. Four years ago, we had a lot of incidents of violence. The tactic was to pull the fire alarm to get everybody outside, so they could jump people on the way back in. I mean, I saw a kid get his head thrown through a plate glass window. You know, metal detectors aren't gonna stop that. All of that was mostly gang related.

That was four years ago. None of that is going on but, then again, our population has declined greatly. Principal Kittle has been instrumental in making sure that everyone knows that this is not where you come and do that kind of business. But, the kids still spend so much energy focused on the sociology and psychology of gangs.

Here's a really good example of what I mean—we have spirit day every other week. We wear stuff from our state and local universities to promote college-going. And then, on other Fridays we wear something Huerta spirit-oriented. I have a red jersey with Dolores Huerta's initials on it. When I wear that, kids are like, 'Oh, you're representing that clique.'

I instantly let them know that they need to understand that people come from a world where nobody cares about this gang or that gang. There's a whole world out there where that doesn't even exist. I tell them that they need to focus on what's on the back of the jersey, what Dolores Huerta stands for and how she lives her life. It's not about the way these colors have been adopted by a gang organization. The kids look at me like *I* don't understand because I'm White and not from around here. I get their perspective intellectually, but in my heart, I just don't.

When there's a gang incident at this school, it almost makes me laugh. A lot of our kids don't respond to counseling. It's like our kids are just so submerged in violence and discord and dysfunction that unfortunately they kind of just take it all with a grain of salt. They experience o much violence in their everyday that it's normalized. It takes something really big for them to be shocked.

Now, what happened at Fenger High School with Derrion Albert, that's on another scale. There are certainly tears and sad expressions, but it's like when certain things happen, kids are just like, 'Oh well, there goes another.' They're like, 'Well, you don't understand. You don't know what it's like.' And, I don't. I don't live on the west side. I live on the northwest side. I live in a very nice middle-class neighborhood.

Truth be told, I had to escape gentrification myself, so I do understand what it's like to be displaced and to be pushed further and further and further. But, I don't understand what it's like to be in fear every time I walk out my front door. That I don't get and I'm not going to try and tell them that I know what that's like.

It's baffled me for years the way Chicago is and everybody's so racially isolated. The school closings don't help either. It makes things more difficult to get away from. I think kids here reach some sort of place where they know that I care and that my lack of understanding their day-to-day stuff shouldn't matter. That's a professional challenge for me, and even for the teachers. It never goes away.

Some of the root causes adding to the violence our kids face is entrenched poverty. It's no way to live. Something that struck me that I've finally learned when I talk to kids is that I don't ask them where they live. I ask them where they stay because that's the word that they use. I think they feel a sense of rootlessness like, 'We're here now, but we could get evicted' or 'We're staying with my auntie but we might have to move somewhere else soon.' I can't even imagine what that's like. Having a degree in developmental psychology and a master's in counseling, I know how important a sense of security is. How can you have that if you don't know where you're going to be sleeping from night to night? That's certainly one root cause.

Another root cause comes from an interesting experience I just had today. One of my kids that graduated two years ago came to visit me. She brought her 14-month-old son, Anthony, who I refer to as my grandson because the student used to call me 'momma.' It was funny when she told me she was pregnant. I told her that the situation happened, it's done, we need to move on, and we need to plan for your future and your baby's future. She said, 'I was more worried to tell you than to tell my mother.'

So, she brought little Anthony in to come see me and he's active and he's running around. He's just a smart little guy. You know, hanging out at a high school, there are no toys here for him to play with and he was getting into my office supplies and she kept slapping him. Not hard, but still hitting him. I think there's just that in some students' lives, from day one, everything's solved with violence. Even when they were leaving, I bent down to tie his shoe and he just kind of slapped me in the cheek, and then she hit him.

It's like there's this literal cycle there. I said, 'Honey, come on. I don't mean to tell you what to do, but you can't keep hitting him for everything. He's just being a baby.' When she called me the other day and I told her to come see me. I asked her, 'How's my little man doing?' She goes, 'Oh, he's bad.' And that's what you hear from these young moms over and over again and again, 'Oh he's so bad.' When they're infants, it's all good because they can just hold them. But as soon as they start doing baby things like walking around, they always get a smack and a hit. Maybe that's part of it.

These kids just lead such isolated lives. All they ever see is kids just like them. A lot of times there's no father around. Mom's working two or three jobs just barely making ends meet. Every time a kid has their parent come, parents are like, 'I had to take a day off work to be here and I could lose my job.' All the time you hear this: 'I may lose my job. I'm not coming in again. I'm gonna lose my job if I take another day off.' These young parents have that tenuous existence. The level of stress has got to be overwhelming.

Another root cause is gentrification. We had something similar to Fenger four years ago when they started to close Austin High School. They [CPS] would send kids to this school, which is kind of what happened at Fenger. Students were trying to establish, 'Well I'm from here and I'm from there.' That's what a lot of kids said with the Fenger situation. It wasn't necessarily all gang related. It was territorial outside of the gang. 'I'm from here and I gotta show people how tough we are on this street.' You know, kids' whole sense of themselves is tied up in where they're from and that no one is going to take anything from them.

I've lived in the Chicago area my whole life and I've only worked in Chicago public schools. I mean, Chicago is so segregated. I think more than just about any other established city. I was in Detroit this summer. Even as decimated as Detroit is, I was surprised by how diverse it was compared to Chicago. I think that's part of it. I think especially if you go to the west side all those vacant lots are still there after the riots, after Dr. King was shot. I can't imagine what seeing bleakness every day does to somebody.

At the same time, these kids have such pride in where they come from, which you can't fault. But, they need a way to channel their pride into positive energy, into building something up for the community rather than fighting with other kids from another community to show how tough they are. It's a literal cycle of violence.

What's a really interesting phenomenon is that whenever there's the hint of a fight going on, everybody will run to go see. Rather than standing back saying, 'Hey let's not go. We don't want to get pulled into it too.' Students run towards it, so there's a fascination with it. This seems to happen more with young women than young men, but just this need for drama and discord. It's just so interesting. On some level, they need another frame of reference for conflict management or resolution. This goes back to what I was saying about being slapped and hit as when you're a young child. That's how you're controlled. As you grow up and learn to manipulate and control your environment, that's what you learn to use.

I think it's very, very interesting. We need to step back from what we think is the horror of it and look at it as a disease. If we can depersonalize it, that will actually make it easier to deal with. You need to look at violence like tuberculosis rather than saying it's the children. The problem is when we get emotionally involved in it. That's where people are so busy arguing about the emotion of it that they can't deal with the real issue. We have to look at all the different factors involved, the gentrification, the dislocation, the creation of these ghettos and find a way to discuss this where it doesn't become so charged.

Look at this Fox News versus MSNBC world that we live in. I just love looking at the comments in the *Tribune* or whatever. It's like nobody ever ends up talking about what the article is about. They just end up screaming at each other about being a liberal or a conservative. We need to get away from that because it's not the answer. The problem still remains no matter how many Democrats or Republicans were in office a given year. We need to find a way to have meaningful discourse about how we're actually going to be able to help these kids on a practical level, on a clinical level.

Huerta has all this school security—another Band-Aid. I don't even know if it really makes kids feel more secure. I think it almost makes them feel like they're not trusted. I've had that talk with some kids and they don't always understand that a lot of the policing they see comes from policy above the school. It's not the principal or teachers who always want more security. It comes from the Board of Education and the mayor.

If safety was really the focus at this school, then we need to look at the structure of the building. I know when we were doing small schools and it was adequately funded, we had enough positions that we could have the correct structure in place and promote the whole idea of personalization. Kids knew there was a core group of adults that cared about them. They knew we got together once a week and had meetings and discussed what was going on.

There was a whole different sense in that school. Even though it was still a huge school building, you had these little small learning communities within that building. When it was, there was a brief shining golden moment that seemed like we could turn things around.

Then, the powers that be decided that it just wasn't going work. On top of that, I don't know the exact sequence of events, but then Austin kids came in. Interestingly enough, when Arne Duncan had an interview with *Chicago Magazine* on his way out of town last January, he said that dismantling those schools and dispersing all those kids was his one regret. It's like well, that's really great, after you've destroyed all these schools and all these lives.

I've been following the Comer School movement. The whole idea is that the school is a community center. Yes, while we recognize that there are these deficits in the neighborhood, the child and his family can come into the school and receive an array of services that all support the child's ability to be in school and function in school. I wrote my master's thesis about chronic community violence. The literature is all about how this affects kids' ability to learn and what protective factors of resilience are out there that will help a kid be able to deal with this. It wasn't necessarily a family member, but there was some adult that every one of those kids could depend on.

That's the thing that is so sad about Renaissance 2010 and the disruption and closing of schools. We have to let the kids continue. The school may be the only stable thing in their life. There needs to be political will and a better way to address school failure than just firing and displacing everybody. Just look at Huerta. Our test scores are not great. They've been pretty much flat over the last few years. We've got some remarkable teachers and we have some that need to pursue other opportunities [giggles], but that is the structure that we have to deal with.

We've also have a very strong teacher's union. The problem is that nobody's focusing on what's really important which are the kids. Everybody's dancing around each other trying to get what's best for the adults. The kids don't even come into the equation. Kids are at the bottom and all the adults are looking up.

What I would like to see is a school that truly, truly serves the children. The children are at the center with adults empowered to serve the children. There's not all this top-down policy with testing, accountability and assessment. Yes, that's very important, but more testing is not going to improve a school. It's not going to improve the life of a kid who may have walked to school, comes in shaking because he's been out at 4 in the morning running around with his gang buddies and saw somebody get shot and their brains ended up on his shoulder. He needs to know that he is safe at school and that his school will be there for him and it's not going anywhere.

It really disturbs me when people say that these kids are animals. No. There are kids that have been subjected to some really awful, horrible stuff. It's the kind of stuff that we, as adults, would probably keel over and have a heart attack if we had to deal with it. If they don't have full-blown post-traumatic stress disorder, they have post-traumatic stress syndrome, which is subclinical. They're not quite there yet. It's kind of like the mosquito in your ear. It's just always there.

You know, medical research has done CAT scans, MRIs and blood tests. These kids' cortisol levels are through the roof. Fight and flight response is always kicked in. So, that's where they're starting. That's their baseline. How do you come to school and how do you focus when that's where you are, when you may not have slept, when you may have had to be riding around on the 'El' all night, when somebody says something to you and you're going to snap? I just think about how snappish I am when I don't get a good night's sleep. I can't even imagine what everyday life is like for them.

November 2009

YEAR 2009:

QUESTIONS, REFLECTIONS & RESOURCES

Questions/Reflections

When public schools like Huerta institute jailhouse effects, this response is usually based on America's persistent idée fixe with security technologies as a method for assuaging mass perceptions of schools as dangerous places, induced by the wake of highly publicized school shootings in areas such as Pearl, Mississippi; Paducah, Kentucky; Jonesboro, Arkansas; Columbine, Colorado; and Newtown, Connecticut.

A glaring fact that is often ignored, however, is that most of the violence that students encounter does not occur inside of schools, but rather on the way to and from them. Reported FBI statistics have shown that arrest rates amongst juveniles for violent crimes—aggravated assault, robbery, rape and murder—significantly declined in 1994 and continued to drop through 2019. Despite this, public fears of students being murdered at school have caused considerable anxiety, compelling school districts across the U.S. to pour millions of tax dollars into security technology and armed guards.

School shootings are statistically rare events in comparison with the risk of murders that are more likely to happen outside of classrooms and hallways. Over the past decade, Center for Disease Control (CDC) research on youth homicides has found that an average of more than two dozen school-age children were murdered every week in the U.S., but only about 1% of those killings took place inside schools.

I recognize that for parents, teachers, principals, and youth across the country, safety is a leading priority for learning to occur at an optimal level. This makes sense. What I take issue with, however, is how the often unquestioned pervasiveness of such technologies come without legal protections, while demonstrating the multiple ways in which hyper-securitization exploits the humanity of low-income minority youth at the expense of a majority declared "security for all."

Massive public attention to school shootings, which tragically occurred in predominantly White districts, helped to introduce the 1994 Gun-Free Schools Act. This legislation encouraged states to initiate their own regulatory laws like that of zero tolerance. These policies subsequently coincided with a boost in surveillance technology, SROs and drug sweeps, all of which coincided with the disproportionate punishment of Black and Brown students.

Racialized discrimination within schools has been well-documented by researchers who argue that the misbehaviors of wealthy White students, attending highly-funded learning centers, are more tolerated by authority figures versus the same acts committed by Students of Color in divested schools. This socially unequal cultural experience resulted in higher suspension and expulsion rates among minority youth throughout much of the 2000s. It also sent a clear message that these youngsters had less "value" than their White counterparts, so why should schools and, to a greater extent society, protect or invest in their potential?

The following books, journal articles, websites and other resources help to address the this query, while also compelling us to delve deeper into the social phenomena of gentrification and the social disinvestment of Black futures in America.

Books/Articles

BLACK, D. W. (2018). *Ending zero tolerance: The crisis of absolute school discipline.* New York, NY: New York University Press.

DAY, I. (2015). Being or nothingness: Indigeneity, antiblackness, and settler colonial critique. *Critical Ethnic Studies 1*(2), 102–121.

DU BOIS, W. E. B. (1998). *Black Reconstruction in America, 1860– 1880.* New York, NY: Free Press.

FULLILOVE, M. T. (2016). *Root shock: How tearing up city neighborhoods hurts America, and what we can do about it.* New York, NY: One World/Ballantine Books.

HWANG, J., & SAMPSON, R. J. (June 2014). Divergent pathways of gentrification: Racial inequality and the social order of renewal in Chicago neighborhoods. *American Sociological Review, 79*(4),726–751.

RANSBY, B. (2018). *Making all Black lives matter: Reimagining freedom in the twenty-first century* (First edition). Berkeley, CA: University of California Press.

STOVALL, D. O. (2016). *Born out of struggle: Critical race theory, school creation, and the politics of interruption.* Albany, NY: State University of New York Press.

TAYLOR, K. (2019). *Race for profit: How banks and the real estate industry undermined Black homeownership.* Chapel Hill, NC: The University of North Carolina Press.

TAYLOR, E. (2013). *Surveillance schools: Security, discipline and control in contemporary education*. London, England: Palgrave Macmillan.

Organizational Websites/Other Resources

Chicago Housing Initiative (*www.chicagohousinginitiative.org*) is a coalition of community organizations working with low-income renters in the city of Chicago. Their goal is to advocate and work on behalf of low-income families and seniors to enhance their social, economic and political power.

LUCHA (*www.lucha.org*) was established in 1982 and has presently become a leading Midwest housing advocacy group. It organizes community members to fight for improved housing services in both public and private sectors.

The Resurrection Project (*www.resurrectionproject.org*) addresses growing devastation and crime in the Pilsen neighborhood in Chicago. They work to restore public spaces for housing and other community assets.

Right to the City Alliance (*www.righttothecity.org*) began in 2007 and is a nationally unified alliance based in New York City. Its mission is to highlight gentrification and uprooting practices in urban communities impacting low-income, people of color and LGBTQ residents.

YEAR 2009 NOTES

[1] A pseudonym.

[2] A pseudonym.

[3] A pseudonym.

[4] Austin High School opened in 1876 in the Austin neighborhood of the west side of Chicago. It was named after a Chicago real estate developer Henry W. Austin. Under Ren 2010, Austin was phased out in 2007 due to under-enrollment and low test scores. Its building facility was slowly converted into three smaller high schools over the years—Austin Polytechnical Academy (2007); Austin Business and Entrepreneurship Academy (2006); and V.O.I.S.E. Academy High School (2008). As of 2016, Austin's racial demographics were 84% Black, 4% White, 0.50% Asian, and 0.80% and 10% Latinx.

[5] Edward Beasley Elementary Magnet Academic Center is located on Chicago's south side in the Washington Park neighborhood. The school's student demographics are approximately 97% Black and 2% Latinx with 82% being low-income. As of 2018, Beasley had 1,335 students, grades pre-kindergarten through eighth.

[6] A pseudonym.

[7] A pseudonym.

[8] All CPS dean of students positions exist to ensure a safe and stable school climate, particularly in areas of classroom management,

discipline and restorative justice. According to CPS policy, duties and responsibilities of school deans includes, but is not limited to, working closely with high school principals; developing a clear behavioral and disciplinary framework; managing internal and third-party professional development training; and integrating new and/or strengthening existing programs and resources that support a positive school culture.

[9] CPS's Student Code of Conduct (SCC) is adopted by the Chicago Board of Education every year, clarifying expectations for student behaviors. There are six student behaviors, or code violations, covered in the SCC: 1) inappropriate behaviors; 2) behaviors that disrupt; 3) behaviors that seriously disrupt; 4) behaviors that very seriously disrupt; 5) behaviors that most seriously disrupt; and 6) behaviors that are illegal and most seriously disrupt. The SCC also catalogues the rights and responsibilities of students, parents/guardians, school staff and CPS's Chief Executive Officer.

[10] A pseudonym.

[11] A pseudonym.

[12] A pseudonym.

[13] A pseudonym.

[14] A pseudonym.

[15] A pseudonym.

[16] The Type 75 endorsement, also known as the State of Illinois General Administrative Certificate, was a requirement for educators

seeking the position of assistant principal or principal, assistant or associate superintendent and/or similar positions. Presently, new requirements for principal preparation programs, from admission through endorsement, have replaced the decades-long Type 75 general administrative certificate with a new principal endorsement.

[17]Arne Duncan was appointed by Mayor Richard M. Daley to serve as CPS's Chief Executive Officer in 2001. From 2001 to 2008, Duncan garnered wide political praise for uniting the city's stakeholders in backing Ren 2010. After his tenure in CPS, Duncan went on to serve as President Barack Obama's Secretary of Education.

[18] The disciplinary process, as laid out in CPS's School Code of Conduct (SCC), is "intended" to be instructional and corrective, not punitive. All students are entitled to due process in situations of suspension or expulsion. Decisions in these cases allow parents/guardians of students to appeal any consequence or intervention. As stated in the 2009 SCC manual: "no employee of the Board of Education may inflict corporal punishment of any kind upon persons attending the public schools of the City of Chicago." With that, Chicago's Board of Education must engage in three actions: "(1) create a consistent set of expectations for student behavior for the Chicago Public Schools system and all students; (2) outline the interventions and consequences for students who engage in inappropriate behavior; and (3) reinforce positive behavior and provide students with opportunities to develop appropriate behavioral skills."

[19] Bling-bling, or bling, is a colloquialism popularized by hip hop culture, referring to expensive and flashy jewelry, clothing or other possessions.

[20] A pseudonym.

[21] A pseudonym.

[22] The colloquialism "punked" means being disrespected or humiliated.

[23] "Tweaked" refers to acting stupid or doing something dumb.

[24] A pseudonym.

[25] A pseudonym.

YEAR 2011

"This is a place for education."
DANIEL WATSON[1]

Daniel Watson has been an educator for eight years at Eastman High School.[2] Eastman is located on the far south side of Chicago. Prior to the 1970s, the school's student body was all-White, largely from working class homes. White flight over the past several decades gradually brought more students of color into the school, as well as the surrounding community.

Daniel mostly teaches freshman Algebra, but also instructs higher grades. Not only is he a member of Eastman's Local School Board, but he also runs an after-school program for students across the grades. "The program integrates sports and art into what is essentially a life-skills curriculum. We have students who mainly like the sports part, and that's the hook."

There are some schools where the job title 'dean' is more like the 'top cop' of the school. At Eastman, we call them 'deans' too. They're the ones that handle the discipline of the school. So let's say, me as a teacher, I refer a student who is insubordinate to me. I write the referral and send it down to the dean. The dean then goes through due process with the student to make sure they understand what they did wrong, have a chance for rebuttal, and then pass out the punishment, whether it be an out of school suspension or an after-school suspension. After-school detention means a call to the house to let them know what's happening.

So, we have about three deans and about five dean assistants. The dean assistants are there to help the deans and to patrol the building. We also have a police liaison officer and that's it. Most of our security, as far as personnel are concerned, is the teachers themselves. We do have security cameras, pretty much in every hallway, lunchroom, entrances, but obviously not in the classroom, but everywhere else.

Security cameras are just one of those things that gets rid of the hearsay, you know? Students say, 'Well, this is what happened. Blah, blah, blah.' Cameras just eliminate all of that. Here's the evidence. Like I said, as part of the due process, 'Here's the evidence we have against you. You said this is what happened, but if we look at the video, you can see that you clearly were the one instigating it.' If no teacher was around a zone where maybe students were at a particular time, then we can go to the cameras to get a better understanding of what exactly happened.

For instance, this young lady thought her book bag had got stolen. So, she reported it to me. She was like, 'Hey, my book bag got stolen.' I'm like, 'Okay, did you have it from the beginning of the day?' She said, 'Yeah.' So, we went back to the camera feed and we looked at the beginning of the day all the way up until where she thought it was stolen. It wasn't that far in the day and she never had the book bag. So, it's just little things like that where you actually never brought in the bag. Come to find out her mother had it. So, the cameras are used for things of that nature or even fights.

If you see a fight, maybe you didn't catch one person who threw a punch because you're too busy trying to break it up. You don't see everybody who's involved in the actual altercation. Just things like that. Like I said, arguments, maybe a food fight where you want to catch the people who did certain things. Other than that, the cameras aren't used for too much else. It's just another way just to get the story from besides the student. You look at the cameras to say, 'Okay everybody, it's pretty much lining up the way that people say that it did happen.' So it's just like, to verify.

A lot of Chicago public schools use metal archways and scanning machines. There's none of that here. Nothing against the schools that have it, but I just think, for me personally, once you start bringing those things in, you pretty much have lost already. If it's getting to the point where you have to install metal detectors, then there are some bigger issues that probably need to be addressed other than what metal detectors do. This isn't a huge crime area like, I guess, some other schools have to deal with. Our students pretty much kind of know what to expect when they're here. We just think schools should be one of the safest places for a kid.

Eastman didn't really need all the money attached to local and federal policies like from the Gun-Free Safe Schools Act.[3] With that Act, a lot of schools were given federal dollars to bring in security equipment that would be tailored to their particular needs. So, schools would be like, 'We need the cameras, but we really don't need the metal detectors. We'll get the metal detectors because we get extra funds, but we'll just put the metal detectors to the side *or* we do need more security, more cameras, and such.'

I just don't think you want to set up an environment where you got kids thinking about policing. You want kids to be focused on their education. This is a place for education. When they come in and start having to walk through metal detectors, they start thinking, 'Okay, is this Beirut that I'm walking up into or is this a place of learning?' You want them focused on their minds, not invading their privacy to such an extent.

When students come in here, we require them to swipe their IDs. If they don't have an ID, then they have to stand to the side and get a temporary ID. That's one of the things that we establish to make sure that you belong in the school. Once it's determined that you belong in the school, you know what we expect. We depend on students and teachers to pretty much keep an eye out. So, students will come up to you at any given point and say, 'Hey, you know what, this is what's going on. Such and such might have this.' You know, students want to be safe, so they'll let you know right off the bat.

In the eight years I've been here, I've probably seen two knives that students have carried in. One was an Honors student and one was a Special Education student. Both of them said the same thing: 'It has nothing to do with school, but on the way home.' So, it's not so much violence within the school that they're concerned about. It's outside of school, trying to make it home safely.

That's the big issue right there. I don't think it's violence in a school that you're ever going to not prevent. When students are in school, I don't think that's their major issue. They know they're safe as long as they're in the confines of this building. Once they leave, I think that's where the biggest fears come into play.

I do know we had a problem in the last few years with these made-up, wannabe gangs that they [students] formed. When I say 'made-up,' I think it was unique to our city. You know, back in the day we had the same thing when I was younger, with everybody who lived in Bronzeville versus everybody who lived in Washington Park. We would fight each other, but we were all friends. We were on our school's football teams. It was just an extension of that relationship. Whereas these students today, they have real animosity towards each other. They think it means something beyond this side of the street. They would actually kill each other if it became too intense.

So now, you got all these different wannabe gangs out there, which started about four or five years ago and it's gotten pretty crazy. It seems like every single day one person is getting mixed up with the other person's group or something like that. You still have legitimate gangs, trust me. I mean, *this is Chicago*. You still have gangbangers and all those issues. But, there are a lot of people that obviously got kicked out of Ida B[4] and the Robert Taylor[5] projects and moved further south to us. So, I think this area is becoming new turf.

The new students coming in, I believe, have to feel safer than where they were at. I say this for a couple of reasons. One, if students do argue or fight inside the school, they know it's gonna get broken up immediately. Whereas, two, if they're outside, there's no telling when or if anybody would ever break it up. So, I believe that they know that they're safe here, which is why they don't do some of the things in here that they would do outside the confines of this building. They know.

If students are gonna fight, it would only make sense to fight outside. You know? If they really wanted to fight each other, they'd do it outside because they know won't nobody break it up. I don't care who's around. They know nobody's going to break it up. Inside, you'll see kids start arguing, getting loud and doing all those things before they start fighting. But, they don't get to that point because they know that a teacher's about to walk up at any moment. They know they only got five seconds to start fighting and then it's getting broken up. As soon as a teacher gets there, they typically stop fighting.

So, new students, and even our old ones, absolutely feel safe. This is why, if you do see a fight brewing, it happens because they know that this is a safe place. They can waste time huffing and puffing because they know that it's going to get broken up and nobody's gonna get hurt. This is where they come to bring their issues because they know, in the end, I'm gonna be able to go back home. If I fight outside, there's no guarantee I'm getting back home safe. There's no guarantee that somebody won't jump me or something like that.

While Eastman has its expectations, we also have a zero tolerance for certain things. Two fights and you're gone. You might have that one fight, but if you fight again, you're basically not here for an education. So, you need to just go ahead and find you another place to go to school. It's those things like that. We sit here, you argued, we mediated, you agreed to stop fighting, we had peer mediators all around. We make sure when we see an argument, students can talk it out and we let them know, 'Now it's up to you.' If it goes beyond this point, now we start talking about suspensions and all these other things. There's not a lot of wiggle room.

We let our students know what we expect and if you don't want to be here, that's perfectly fine. You got to go home. That's pretty much how it goes. We make sure we scare them. We let them know and show examples. Like, one time I remember there was a fight and the principal let all students know: 'Look, these people that you saw fighting will no longer be here.' He stated over the intercom, 'Just so we're all clear about what we expect.' When you say things like, students start to listen.

That reminds me of school conditions. So, when students walk into this school, they know there's a value here. I have value in this space. I *feel* valued in this space, but it's also a valuable space because this is the key to my future. It's what you allow your students to walk into. That's a different kind of expectation without any zero tolerance policy or adult actually standing over you.

Inside our building, there's no paper lying around. The grass outside is manicured. Maintenance does a wonderful job here. If there's something on the desk, it's gone the next day. The rooms are nice and neat every single time. In my class, students leave with all their stuff. There's no paper on the floor. You take your books with you. The lockers are clean. The floors are always clean and the bathrooms are always neat. So, students come into an environment that says, 'We value you. We're gonna keep it clean for you. Now, you do the same.'

We're constantly showing students that there's all these different programs for them to get into. We have these different avenues for them to take. You don't have to fight. You can do this after school. You don't have to immediately go home. Not only do we have sports, we got all of these different activities you can be doing. There are different things that you can do besides going home. You're having trouble with your homework? There's all these after-school programs you can get into regarding your homework. Those things absolutely matter to a kid.

If there's any changes that I would make to security at Eastman, it would probably be with our teachers. Obviously, students are going to be students. They're going to do what they do. I think you grab those students. I think they will adapt to the environment they're in. I don't think they'll necessarily bring all the hell that comes with them. Some students do and those students don't last. Those students leave. But, for the most part, the students that come in, they recognize that the things they used to do elsewhere, won't work in this school. Once they realize it doesn't work, they adapt. Some learn slowly, some learn pretty quickly, but they all learn eventually. Teachers need to understand that.

For the most part, I try to handle issues on my own. I stand in the back of the room. I'm gonna try to keep you in this classroom. I'm not going to call the dean and have you kicked out. I don't put my kids out in the hall. If he talks, I give him a zero. He knows that's fair. Then, I see him not talking. He's not doing anything because he understands that this is a moment. This is his grace period right now. I'm allowing him to still be in my presence. So, teachers need to be aware and appreciative about a student being quiet. Some teachers go back and forth with students and it just escalates. Where, I'm like there are really no options here. It's my way or we have to figure this out another way like getting your parents involved and up at the school quick.

It all goes back to what I said about school conditions. Some areas are a lot rougher than others. You have to keep that in mind, but I definitely think it's the tone that you set in the building. It's the value that the kids know they have. They need to see new things, additions to the buildings. They can't see that their books and classrooms are just completely worn down. They need to know that teachers have high expectations for them. They know the difference between a good teacher and a bad teacher. They know that somebody somewhere has expectations for them to do well, and they respond to things like that. Without infusing positive attitudes into teachers, I can see why security measures might be necessary.

I know we can't change the attitude of some teachers. We can't change the attitude of some administrators. But, I think that's basically where you have to start. You have to start with administration. You have to start with them and work your way down, from the superintendent to the administrators to the teachers and say, 'This is what's acceptable and this is what's not acceptable, and anything you do outside the realm of making students feel less than human means *you* have to go.' Unfortunately, that's a strict measure, but it's what you have to do to get the desired result.

February 2011

"Consistency is the key."
HELEN McCONNELL[6]

Helen McConnell works with 10th-, 11th- and 12th-grade students at Eastman.[7] For eight years, she has taught General Chemistry, Advanced Placement (AP) Chemistry and Physics. Given school closures in previous years, Helen sees Eastman as a "school of choice for a lot of newly arriving inner-city students." She says that residency issues are a problem for families wanting to enroll into Eastman. "Some students live outside our district, but they still find a way to get into the school."

Security at Eastman, for me, begins with all the doors to the school being locked. Teachers have their own access points but have to use magnetic swipe cards. Students are supposed to come in one door at the beginning of the school day and they're required to scan in. They have an ID and they scan in. If they don't have their ID, they're printed a temporary one.

Every student should enter through the scanning system. The scanning system is a computer where they swipe their card through. It's magnetic. There's a picture of them on their ID and would be on their temporary ID as well, so you can match their face with the picture. With our newer students, those unfamiliar faces, this kind of security is really important.

I'm not exactly sure if these security measures have a purpose. For me personally, they don't. I mean, other than the fact that all the doors are locked then yes, they have a purpose for me. But the students, I think come in other entrances. Instead of coming when they scan, they show up as present.

With the old system, I could tell whether the kid had swiped in to begin with. So when I'm taking attendance first period, I'll say, 'How come you're not highlighted?' Students will say, 'Oh, I don't know.' And I'm like, 'Well, which door did you come in?' They'd say, 'Oh I came in by the band room' or 'I came in through the cafeteria.' But, they can exit the building without swiping. They can leave anytime.

Eastman has no metal detectors. I think that's because the [school] culture that we're trying to perpetuate is that there's no need for metal detectors. We trust our students to be students and we rely a lot on word of mouth if there are any issues. I really haven't been privy to any major instances of weapons or things. I know that there have been some drug instances, but I wouldn't say they're extensive. We do have security cameras, but we rely mainly on the dean's Department of Security. We also have a police officer liaison who's in the building— just one.

In my eight years here, I think the school climate has gotten a little better. I do, especially with the implementation of our Freshman Academy. The freshmen who, for one reason or another, don't attain sophomore status, they go to the Freshman Academy in order to recoup credits to establish sophomore status and then they can come back to their main building. I think that has taken away some of the issues from our main campus where I teach.

When I say 'issues,' I mean gang-related things, the more hard-core, more difficult things. This is the child that's having issues for one reason or another that aren't so much academic, but rather social or behavioral. We have a new building separate from the main, where students that are having trouble adjusting are taken to.

Don't get me wrong. Students are trusted here. We respect them. It's just that we have certain expectations. The expectation of student behavior is such that they have to maintain a certain way of acting. If they don't, our dean's department is very strong and swift to react. Teachers feel very supported by our dean's department and, therefore, the culture is such that students know they need to maintain a certain behavior otherwise they're gonna be sent elsewhere. Our culture is a learning culture, and if you're preventing other students from the learning that they deserve, then you have to be removed.

There's a variety of achievers here. The requirement for my General Chemistry class is you got a C or better in Biology and Algebra. I would say that I have the average student in Chemistry. But then, my AP Chemistry and Physics course has the more higher-achieving students. It can be a mix, depending on what students learned from the school they came from. Trust me—not all schools are created equal [giggles]. I see this every day.

Going back to school security, I often wonder why some schools have police, metal wands and metal detectors, and others do not. I don't know why exactly. Some guesses I could make would be that they don't have a strong, progressive disciplinary plan within their school. Maybe there's a lot of transition in different departments where they don't have a cohesive plan set in place yet. And so therefore, if students don't know there's this plan and everybody should be on the same page, then they're going to try to get away with it as much as they possibly can.

If it's a free-for-all, then that would happen. It could also be within their culture. I mean, if that's how they live in their neighborhood. If there's fighting with different factions, say gangs or even families, then that would carry over into the classroom, as well. And how do you separate that? I don't know. It's a community issue.

Here, we have cameras in our hallways. And, I think our cameras serve a purpose. I think that we don't have metal detectors because maybe there haven't been any major instances within the school building because of our swift actions from the get-go and for years of establishing a culture within our school. We haven't needed them. Maybe other communities haven't had that same culture, so they don't feel safe. Outside the school, there are certainly issues like what you hear on the news, but inside we try to create a different culture and expectation.

If there were any changes that I would make to our school's security, it would just be minor changes. Maybe add just a few more cameras in the parking lot. But, within the school, we feel adequately covered. Also, every now and then, if you hit the call button, sometimes it won't work or somebody's not sitting at the main office desk in order to answer the call button immediately. That would be another change.

Teachers all have call buttons in our room that we can push. It'll cause somebody in the office to come over the intercom and ask what the problem is. We can tell them that we need to have a dean, or need the nurse, or need the principal, or that there's somebody that we have within the classroom that's a problem and needs to be removed.

Regardless of any security changes that I would personally make, it's really about establishing a positive school culture. Our culture is to value students and to get our students to buy into the education portion, not just feel safe. We also want them to achieve and get to know them and create a culture of community that has been very important since I've been here.

I've worked at a parochial school in Savannah, Georgia. I've worked at a Hispanic-Caucasian school in California. I've worked at a very affluent community school in Houston, Texas. From my perspective, kids are kids, and they're the same everywhere I've been. While some of their problems and issues may be different, in different areas, kids are kids. They all want to be accepted and loved and disciplined, so they know the parameters in which they need to work. I find that when there's consistency, they thrive. Consistency is the key. I firmly believe that.

February 2011

"We still have work to do."
JEREMY KING[8]

Jeremy King has served as the principal of George Eastman High School[9] for seven years. He is their first Black school leader. As early as 2005, the school began accepting large numbers of Black and Latinx students from inner sectors of the city experiencing gentrification and school closures. In 2011, the school had approximately 1,600 students with a demographic of 60% Black, 25% Latinx, 15% White, all middle to working class, according to CPS's website. Jeremy feels that he has made necessary and appropriate curricular adjustments to the school given the cultural shifts that Eastman has been witnessing.

We pride ourselves in taking excuses away from education. There's seven computer labs and over 400 computers in the building. There are brand-new science labs and we're starting art smart labs. You can see that the Board [CPS] is invested in the community and in the school, as well. The computer labs are in our relatively new part of the building, about five years old. We put these labs in and now we're putting air conditioning in, as well. We kind of take a lot of the excuses away.

Our school is very clean being that it's old. We do a great job and we give all the credit to the kids. They don't do the graffiti crap. We get a little bit in the washrooms, but you don't see that. So, it's a good place. The kids feel it, recognize it, expect it that way. We put art up throughout the building. We do a lot of visual stuff for the kids, so that's why we got the college flags up there and we try to identify colleges that our kids are accepted to as well as colleges they tend to think about. Our graduation rate is 92% and the acceptance rate is 62–63%. Our dropout rate is about 5%. So, we do lose some kids. Our per-pupil expenditure is about nine grand.

New construction has updated the school from its 1920s and '50s work. One of our gyms is called the Kodak Gym,[10] or the new gym, and again, it's about five years old. It's one of the nicest gyms we think on the south side. Again, the kids take care of it and maintenance takes care of it. We think it's a good place. There's no excuses when you come to this type of school. At other schools, you have all these barriers to success. 'We don't have this. We don't have that.' Here, we really try to make every effort to take excuses out from teaching and learning. So, it's a good place.

We also have what we informally call, 'The Newbie House.' All of our freshmen are in this area. That's why you see the banners that say, 'This is our house.' This is their sanctuary. We try to get them on point. Teachers give them the skills they need before they go into the main building. We have success with kids. Our kids come from four different elementary schools. We have Smith,[11] which is right down the street. We have Forman,[12] we have Kirkland[13] and we have Osler.[14] Four different schools, four different curriculums, four different Boards, four different principals. It's all over the place. It's a good place. We have rooms in the basement. There's another gym over, a weight room and a pool.

We do have new students coming in, but there's not a lot of racial tension. There's definitely no racial tension between Latinos and African Americans. Our biggest struggle is when it comes to discipline between girls—freshman and sophomore girls. You know, it's the biggest struggle that we have when it comes to discipline. We have a fight about once a month. We also lose about twenty kids throughout the year to expulsion for drugs or fighting. Some months are more busy than others. For the most part though, kids go home. But, our female populations are struggling.

At Eastman, we don't have a lot of security measures. We have what's called dean's assistants and we have paraprofessionals, six of them. Six dean's assistants that are all guys who actually kind of assist in the hallways when it comes to passing periods. They work the cafeteria. They're not in uniform or anything like that. We just ask them to wear paraphernalia from the school.

Other than that we have cameras on the perimeter doors and we have cameras in the hallway, about maybe 30–40 cameras throughout the whole building. We put cameras in the gym because we've had some people come in and we want to make sure that when we have strangers in the building, we can identify those people. We do have one police liaison officer, which is through a grant from the city. He's a police officer and he's here every day. Other than that, the security measures are pretty much the people in the building—teachers and administrators.

Our goal is that things happen in the hallways and that's this school. Sixteen hundred kids pass each other and that's when all the activities take place. So, our goal is to get out and about. We [staff and faculty] talk about that when the bell rings. We're out and about. When we got a moment and we're sitting there in a meeting and the bell's about to ring, 'Give me five minutes and we can come back here and restart this meeting' because that's when the activities start. We make it a point to know kids by face and that really does make a difference.

When I first started here, IDs were pushed because of the demographic change. It was masked in safety. You know, 'We don't feel safe. Why don't you feel safe?' But, teachers couldn't articulate that. That's where the IDs came in. Teachers didn't know the kids, so we gave students IDs. Leadership placated, 'We'll give them IDs, if you think that's going to make you feel safe.' Until they [teachers] realized that it really didn't make a difference because they came to know all the kids in their class.

The only way they knew kids in the hallway was to start to recognize faces that are supposed to be in this community. Now, they can see that, whether he has an ID on or not. That's pretty much it. Some kids use it. They can even use it as a credit card. So, it gained more purpose than just for security. I like to think that the security measures here, pretty much, are the people in the building, knowing kids' faces and being out and about.

For me, it's a school's culture that dictates the needs for security measures like metal wands, metal detectors, and so forth. It's about school culture because people in this area probably think we've got the same problems as the inner city. Some people want more of those things [security] here because they think schools are dangerous, some godforsaken place until they walk in here like, 'Oh wow, this is a school?' I think that part of the leadership team and the Superintendent says, 'Look. We want to create a school as opposed to this kind of gateway to a prison, this kind of image of fear. The kids do need to go to school.'

Leadership pushed to have uniforms my first year and we argued back and forth: 'You go to Lane Tech and they don't have uniforms. Why do we have to have uniforms?' Then, that whole debate kind of went away. So, I think that's what makes a difference. Our kids don't wear uniforms. I think what makes a difference here is the school itself, the kids in the building. They respect the place. They respect it because of the culture and climate we try to create.

Now, don't get me wrong. Some kids get nutty and they become disrespectful. Absolutely, they do. But, my philosophy here is that I'm not gonna spend 90% of my time talking about 10% of the kids who are a problem. That means that 90% of the kids aren't the problem, so let's focus on educating that 90% that aren't the problem. The 10% that are going to be a problem? Well, that's not going to change. We'll deal with them. They're gonna get suspended. I'm sorry mom. I'm sorry dad, but my energy's not going to be on that. That's been the mantra that parents and I have talked about a lot, which is difficult sometimes because it weighs on you.

It's important to the kids too. It's something that we told our staff as well and they buy into it. People aren't worried about looking over their shoulders, worried about this community or these kids. That has helped out a lot. We have a creed or a mantra that we say every morning: 'Hardworking, responsible and respectful.' There's a lot of that imagery around the building. You see the walls. You see things that I think kids have subliminally taken with them: 'This is what we can be and here is what we expect.' That makes a big difference.

I think that students feel safe here. We catch kids with marijuana. We caught a kid with a knife this week, but kids tell us. We catch kids doing stupid stuff. We know those kids are obviously not on the same page. But, I think that culture and climate is so important to kids feeling safe. Kids will tell other kids, 'Hey man, don't do that. We don't do that here. They'll put you out.' That's just the theme we set. I'll tell kids, 'I'm the patriarch. I'm being paid to be the patriarch. This is my house. I'm not your mama or your daddy, but in my house these are my rules.' This is how we do stuff. You don't come to work in the gym. You come to go to school.

That's the thing we tell freshmen, and it just keeps going on. I think definitely students feel safe. They know. We had a kid who got in trouble in the neighborhood and a girl who made poor decisions. They got in the middle of things [argument] after school. She came back here at 4:30. We asked what happened and she told the story. We have a social worker here and she was able to talk to her. This community has done a great job of trying to continue to create trust because perception is not based on race.

Creating a school culture is a choice. We had to make a choice. We had to provide reasons for people and show that this can be a safe place. We had to talk about race and culture. When it comes to school shootings, and all this stuff, it doesn't happen in minority schools. So that choice, making those decisions is tough, and I think it's financial. I think it takes away from what we want to do, as far as teach. Making that choice not to have a lot of security was important because we don't want people to say, 'Now, the ownership of making this school safe is on the security guard as opposed to me as a teacher.'

We had a situation last year where two girls were constantly bickering with some other girls. They were from different neighborhoods before they came to Eastman and you know how that goes. Anyway, the bickering was going on and on and on. The parent came in very belligerent and I said, 'Let me tell you something. I don't talk to you that way, so you don't talk to me that way.' She said, 'That's what's wrong with this damn place. You ain't got no security guards.' I said, 'Wait a minute. You're telling me you want your child to go to a school with security guards? Why do you need security guards? What's the security guard going to stop? The behavior of your child? That doesn't do anything. Security guards shouldn't do that. You should control your child.'

That parent started talking about some other school. I said, 'This ain't that place. If that's the type of place that you want, you go back there. This is the type of place we have here. We don't want security guards. We take ownership. We want you to feel safe, but you don't have to come here. If you can't buy into that, you go back.' She was really was pissed off at what I said because she thought more security was the answer to misbehavior. And, I kind of get it. That's how a lot of city schools work, so you get used to it.

I think parents and educators totally miss the link between the impact of security on student learning because they're so used it. They see it as one of the same. It's just immediate and it happens in a number of different ways, especially if you compare us to other places. First of all, a kid gets up in the morning and puts on a uniform. He thinks, 'I'm going to a jail cell. I get up. I get in this uniform. I go to this big building. These are warehouses and I have to go through a metal detector, check my book bag, get patted down by this guy with a gun and a security shirt on.'

That whole imagery is totally contradictory to learning. So now, that student is already violent, already tense, already wound up. He has to wear something that he doesn't want to. He goes through a metal detector because he's not trusted. Then, he walks around knowing 'they' don't even trust me to walk a mile in my own school because I got 'Big Willy' [security guard] over here watching me. Then, I go into class, after that whole thing, and you want me to learn?

The whole concept has nothing to do with learning. No, it has everything to do with learning. It tells you exactly who you are and what you're capable of. I wouldn't work here if that was going to continue because I don't think that's what our kids need. They, or rather we, don't need that type of mentality. It's unfortunate that it's masked sometimes in race. It's masked sometimes in security, but it's still about race. I tell people all the time, 'When this school was all-White 30 years ago, you weren't worried about any of that stuff.'

This school now has a higher graduation rate. We have higher ACT scores. So, what are you saying? It's gotta be something else. You go down the street to Osler. Ain't nobody got a uniform on. Why? 'Oh, it's their socioeconomic status?' But, people here also make a decent income. No question these are things that still weigh on People of Color—Black and Brown.

It's the self-fulfilling prophecy. We've bought into this whole concept that Black people are dangerous and can't be controlled. This is what we implicitly tell kids when schools have a security guard. Then, I become the warden. This dog knows where to sit, so you're an animal. We bought into this concept that students can't be mature, they can't have fun, they have to have a uniform on, they have to do these things. Changing the mindset of people is hard, but Eastman is trying.

To be honest, when people come here they're like, 'Oh, where is the security guard? Where is the metal detector?' I definitely think we stopped seeing it. It's become upon us as educators, at least in this building, to break that mindset and let kids know, 'You're free of those things. You don't have to be put into some box of violence, of uncontrollable nature that you can't be taught unless you are reined in by cops and metal detectors and stuff like that.' We've become accustomed to that.

Kids come here from the south and west sides all the time. Some want to come, others don't. We had a kid who came in and couldn't handle it. He wanted to go back. 'I gotta go back to Farragut,[15]' he said. I said, 'What's the matter?' He said, 'You guys are lame.' I said, 'Why?' We got to talking about Eastman and how he's expected to go to class. I said, 'Dude, that's what you're supposed to do.' I told him that we got nothing but love here, so let's act that way. It was hard for him to do that. He struggled the semester he was here because I know where he came from. He couldn't transition, but that's reality. When you're caught up in those spaces, where you're always locked down, it's almost preferred over liberation.

My advice for schools about what they can do to change the reality of moving past lockdown is that your leadership has to be strong. We have to be leaders and set clear expectations for kids. Kids have been screwed up. They're not screwed up because of what they do. They're screwed up because of adults. We are taking advantage, taking things away from them and we're not giving them the building blocks they need. Some of those things are economically based and kids are at a disadvantage. While adults still need to be who we are, we still need expectations for kids. I think schools' leaders have to set a strong culture of expectation in their building. Say what's going to be accepted and not accepted in their building and hold to that.

Kids will rise to the occasion. I can tell you that it's happened in this building. It even happened when I was at Proviso East.[16] We kept pushing the agenda: 'This is who we are. This is the school.' We weren't running a this-and-that asylum. We changed the culture for kids and, in turn, we changed the culture with teachers because the fear is there. We talked about what it means to be free of that. We said, 'They're [Black youth] not dangerous, just loud. Tell them to shut up and move on.' I think by continuing to set those expectations with your faculty and with your student body makes a hell of a difference about who kids are and what kids respond to.

It's crazy that there's 1,600 kids in here and only 100 of us [staff and faculty], but we can run this. We have to because we believe kids will buy into what the adults say if they see the system is working in a fair way. We talk to them, hold them accountable. You still got to study. You still got to do these things. I think school leaders have to do a better job of that. We still have work to do. If I go to another school, it would be the same thing because it's important and it's necessary.

February 2011

YEAR 2011:

QUESTIONS, REFLECTIONS & RESOURCES

Questions/Reflections

From this last yearly section, one of the key standout statements was by Daniel Watson: "It's the value that the kids know they have." From him and his colleagues, themes such as "respect," "hard work," "trust" and "responsibility" repeatedly emerged—language that was also part of Eastman's daily mantra. As more than mere rhetoric however, I felt a genuine sense being at this school that teachers, administrators and even students were genuinely working towards making the above tenets real through the minimization of school security and the maximization of communal trust and personal value.

So, what does creating student value further entail beyond what Eastman was trying to achieve? More to the point, what should the immediate intents of this be within the context of ultra-securitized, hypersegregated schools? If the honest goal is to recognize and then to disrupt the real and symbolic institutional violence that Students of Color experience, then at least two necessary components come to mind: The first, as previously stated, calls for teachers and staff to engage in deep, reflective analyses of their own implicit biases around race, class and gender; the second requires us to rethink and restructure school spaces, curriculum and policies to be more representative and ethical for Students of Color.

With respect to the first point, tightly held conscious and unconscious cultural fallacies and labels must be dispelled and dislodged on the road to achieving the second point. Research affirms that student behaviors, socially and academically, are influenced by microaggressions—subtle, and sometimes not so subtle, messages from teachers about students' self-worth, intelligences, abilities and culture.

Eastman's principal, Jeremy King, discusses how the effects of school culture can be a self-fulfilling prophecy, either negatively or positively. Young people are intuitively aware of how they are perceived and treated in their daily interactions with educators. Thus, establishing and maintaining clear cultural perceptions and high educational expectations of minority youth is crucial in helping them to protect their self-esteem, and thereby reaching their full potential, while also forming learning spaces devoid of discriminatory policies, practices, curriculum and outcomes.

Scholars have long studied the economic and social norms that schools often unknowingly teach—political socialization, transmission of cultural values, training in docility and obedience, and perpetuation of the status quo. Such norms can be found in textbooks that omit vital histories of Black and Latinx peoples (during and prior to European subjugation); in subpar curriculum that positions struggling minority youth behind advanced placement students in preparation for higher learning; in dominant social mores that discount ethnic cultural values of any significance or deem them as an aberration; and, of course, in structural processes that wrongly label Peoples of Color as "oppositional," "deficient" or "untreatable" and in need of removal from schools.

Concerning the second point, parents and educators of 2020 and beyond must absolutely adopt a firm commitment to ridding their schools of the above norms by constructing detailed policies that embrace newer visions of what liberatory education can look like without bodily regulation and that can progressively transform school curriculum and spaces into ones where educators come to know the range of out-of-school issues impacting students and how to reach and elevate them. By engaging in multilateral discussions with students, parents, social workers and counselors, educators can come to see root causes of why young folk are struggling or acting out in classrooms and in neighborhoods.

Disrupting school norms is certainly not a quick fix, nor a panacea. For the short and long haul in doping this kind of work, we need to be conscious, ethical and responsive if we truly desire to see Black and Latinx students rise far beyond racist deficit models and authoritarian protocols that position them as disposable property within a White supremacist system.

In furthering our individual and collective perceptions and efforts on policies and practices that genuinely address liberatory education for Students of Color, I highly suggest the following list of readings and resources.

Books/Articles

ADAMS, M., BLUMENFELD, W. J., CASTAÑEDA, C., HACKMAN, H. W., PETERS, M. L., & ZÚÑIGA, X. (Eds.). (2013). *Readings for diversity and social justice*. New York, NY: Routledge Taylor & Francis Group.

ADAMS, M., BELL, L. A., & GRIFFIN, P. (2007). *Teaching for diversity and social justice*. New York, NY: Routledge.

EMDIN, C. (2016). *For white folks who teach in the 'hood and the rest of y'all too: Reality pedagogy and urban education*. Boston, MA: Beacon Press.

FREIRE, P. (2000). *Pedagogy of the oppressed (30th Anniversary Edition)*. New York, NY: Continuum.

LOEWEN, J. W. (2018). *Lies my teacher told me: Everything your American history textbook got wrong*. New York, NY: The New Press.

MILNER, H. R., & LAUGHTER, J. C. (2015). But good intentions are not enough: Preparing teachers to center race and poverty. *Urban Review: Issues and Ideas in Public Education, 47*(2), 341–363.

MOORE, E., ALI, M., & PENICK-PARKS, M. W. (2018). *The guide for white women who teach Black boys*. Thousand Oaks, CA: Corwin Press.

RUBIN, D. I. (June 2014). Engaging Latino/a students in the secondary English classroom: A step toward breaking the school-to-prison pipeline. *Journal of Latinos and Education, 13*(3), 222–230.

Saad, L. (2020). *Me and white supremacy: How to recognise your privilege, combat racism and change the world.* London, England: Quercus.

Shange, S. (2019). *Progressive dystopia: Abolition, antiblackness, and schooling in San Francisco.* Durham, NC: Duke University Press.

Organizational Websites/Other Resources

Association for Supervision and Curriculum Development (*www.ascd.org*) is an international organization with over 100,000 members—superintendents, principals, teachers and advocates from over 100 countries—focused on helping members and non-members achieve excellence in classrooms and schools.

Dignity in Schools (*www.dignityinschools.org)* is a national coalition designed to confront and dismantle the systemic problem of pushout and school-to-prison pipeline methods occurring in schools.

National Education Association (*www.nea.org*) is America's largest professional organization committed to advancing the cause of public education. This site provides articles and toolkits for teachers on a number of classroom issues and concerns.

Rethinking Schools (*www.rethinkingschools.org*) is a small nonprofit activist publication that presents articles based in classroom practice and educational theory. It is directed by editors and editorial associates who publish works by teachers, parents and students.

YEAR 2011 NOTES

[1] A pseudonym.

[2] A pseudonym.

[3] The Gun-Free Schools Act (GFSA), signed into law by President Bill Clinton on March 31, 1994, was part of a broader federal initiative to improve US schools. As a part of GFSA, states receiving federal funds were required to establish laws regarding firearms. Public schools were also to mandate the removal or expulsion of any student bringing a firearm to school for a period of not less than twelve months. Only the school's chief administrator could modify the punishment.

[4] The Ida B. Wells Homes (or colloquially "the Ida Bs") were a series of two- and three-story row CHA houses sitting on 47 acres of land. This public housing project was located in the Bronzeville community, bordered by Dr. Martin Luther King Drive on the west, Cottage Grove Avenue to the east, 37th Street to the north, and 39th Street (Pershing Road) to the south. The original name of the projects was the South Parkway Garden Homes, but before construction it was renamed the "Ida B. Wells Homes" in June of 1939, after Ida B. Wells who was a Black civil rights activist. Demolition of the Ida B. Wells Homes began in late 2002 and was completed in August 2011.

[5] The Robert Taylor Homes was a CHA public housing project in Bronzeville located on Chicago's south side, stretching from 39th to 54th Street along the Dan Ryan Expressway. The project was named

after Robert Rochon Taylor, a community activist and the first Black chairman of CHA. The homes comprised twenty-eight 16-story buildings, containing nearly 4,300 apartments and 27,000 people. In 1993, the housing authority began moving residents into other areas of the city with the intent of transforming Robert Taylor into mixed-income housing units. Residents were gradually moved out by 2005 with the final building demolished in 2007.

[6] A pseudonym.

[7] A pseudonym.

[8] A pseudonym.

[9] A pseudonym.

[10] A pseudonym.

[11] A pseudonym.

[12] A pseudonym.

[13] A pseudonym.

[14] A pseudonym.

[15] Farragut High School, now known as Farragut Career Academy, is a four-year public high school located in the Little Village neighborhood on Chicago's west side. Named after David Farragut, a naval hero of the American Civil War, the school historically, in the 1960s, was majority Black (over 80%) prior to Ren 2010. Today, Farragut's student

demographic is roughly 13% Black and 87% Latinx with almost 100% being low-income.

[16] Proviso East High School, in District 209, is a four-year public secondary school. It is located in Maywood, Illinois, a western suburb just outside Chicago. Proviso East serves three other suburban villages: Broadview, Forest Park and Melrose Park. The school's total minority enrollment is 97% (50% Latinx and 47% Black) with 63% economically disadvantaged. Proviso East High School is one of three high schools in its district.

OUTRO

Always on Lockdown: An Oral History of Policing and Discipline Inside Public Schools is a collection of peoples' experiences attempting to make sense of their lives, as well as their livelihoods, in an era of intense urban renewal, school closings and ultra-policing. The narratives within this book have an influence to them. They help us recall, recognize and remain aware of the intimate ways in which school participants had to live out the devastating impacts of neoliberal social displacement policies that were not of their own making then and still not today.

For me, what renders this book's narratives especially vital (past and present) is that they reveal and speak to the connective tissue of racism/classism/sexism/colorism in American life that is often left unquestioned, ignored or forgotten. *Always on Lockdown* is not a simple musing of another moment in time. More distinctly, this text serves as a reference and a framework for grasping how marriages between public and private sectors produce conditions of social neglect leading to residential unrest. Likewise, we can take from these lived accounts critical knowledge about our past mistakes and what is needed to build a more egalitarian and humane future for Peoples of Color.

All of the participants in this book, whether they realized it or not (and most did), faced daily normalized societal violence in multiple forms—from residential armed conflicts and gang violence to the police patrolling of schools and neighborhoods; and from hypersegregation and community disinvestment to racial profiling and disproportionate school suspensions and expulsions.

If Chicago public schools are demonstrative of the greater society (and I argue that they are), then what unspoken lessons are other social institutions teaching, or not teaching, young people about surveillance and discipline of their bodies? I will tell you this: Public schools, by and large, do not explicitly teach that the normalization of violence against Black and Brown peoples is dictated by "White supremacist patriarchy" that propagates Whiteness as the dominant hegemonic norm by which all other ethnic groups are judged—whether through institutional policies, discourse and conduct, or symbolic binaries (overt or covert messages such as white plus light equals good and black plus dark equals evil).

Borne out of intersections of policy/discourse/conduct/binaries are recursive and distorted stereotypes of Black and Latinx peoples as "carnal," "violent," "criminal" and "expendable." The internalization of implicit and explicit biases guides the hand of judgment. Thus, how broader society perceives folk of color dictates how they are socially and institutionally treated, how they are condemned, how they are disciplined, and if still alive after this point, how they should be rehabilitated.

This systemic exploitation is nothing new. It's as old as rain. In the American context, it began with the colonization of Indigenous Peoples of Color, combined with the transatlantic slave trade. The objectification and propertization of human bodies post-Emancipation was unlimited through decades of policies and practices like Jim Crow, Black Codes, sharecropping, terror lynching, race riots, "separate but equal" public and private facilities, Nixon's avowed War on Drugs, which later became Clinton's war, then Bush's war, and so forth.

And so, how is this long history of racial marginalization and denigration any different today? The short answer is: *There is no difference.* Peoples of Color, to this very moment, still endure being regulated, exploited and slaughtered; our bodies still overworked, undervalued and dehumanized. Again, drawing historical connections to this present is critical because it can assist younger generations in what will be, by all accounts, future fights against racial injustice and inequality.

Looking back, I must admit that I loathed schooling growing up. Not all aspects of it for sure. I did enjoy learning topics relevant to my culture when it was accurately taught. However, there were lessons—monocultural texts, morals, and procedures—that I intuitively felt were somehow designed to rework, if not reduce, my psychic, intellectual and physical capacities as a young, Black male. Based on national statistics and extensive educational research over the past four decades, I have come to realize that my schooling experiences were far from singular.

Nearly two generations later after high school, I don't see much curriculum advancement in the way that schools presently teach students, except that "Officer Friendly" now looms at the front entrance, electronically wands bodies and book bags, and has license to take young people into custody for merely donning a baseball cap, wearing saggy jeans, or arguing with a teacher or another student.

While currently some U.S. states have ushered in gentler, more equitable policies and measures to address student infractions, mostly in the form of restorative justice programs, a disproportionate number of Black and Latinx youth are still suspended, expelled or treated as disposable versus their White counterparts. Even in major cities like Chicago, Houston and Los Angeles, city halls continue to set aside hefty percentages of their budgets for policing, which can have negative impacts on majority-minority schools and neighborhoods as this book has clearly shown.

Recent protests spurred by the police killings of Breonna Taylor, George Floyd, Tony McDade, Natasha McKenna and many other Black peoples worldwide have re-centered debates on racial injustice in the public consciousness, stimulating discussion around what to do about community policing. While it is agreed upon that schools need to be safe spaces where youth can focus on the main task of learning, differing opinions on the role of cops exist across a broad spectrum: At one end, a strong public and political push for increasing law enforcement as a result of school shootings; at the other end, an equally vehement call for defunding police departments or abolishing their military-style presence altogether (as acutely seen in disadvantaged urban neighborhoods) for the sake of the psychological and physical well-being of community residents, particularly youth.

It's difficult for many people to distinguish between the social poison and the cure, particularly if they're not *woke* to the ways in which the American school system functions or if we fail to listen and recognize how this system is optimally designed for efficiency and control versus free thinking and bodily freedom.

Liberals and conservatives alike believe that to deal with school and community violence, the enlistment of more cops is the definitive answer. This is akin to witnessing someone being repeatedly stabbed and concluding that their wounds only require a Band-Aid. That logic is absurd. It is obviously the stabbing that must first come to a halt through a deep analysis of oppressive conditions and an end to (re)creating them. The violence and trauma within Black urban communities is no doubt an outcome of centuries of being "stabbed" by police incursion; by economic disinvestment in areas of employment, housing and educational opportunities; and, most certainly, by being perceived and treated as less than fully human with little to no rights accorded in spite of the U.S. Constitution.

Whatever progress comes out of current protests around police violence, America will still have an exceedingly long way to go. Indeed, the overuse of law enforcement has become the country's quick fix for dealing with disorder and replacing the heavy lifting of scrutinizing larger systemic factors linked to race, class and gender divisions. In our reliance on school security as a panacea for broader societal violence, are we not simply, as Mary Taylor suggests in her 2009 interview, "treating the symptom rather than the cause of the disease"?

In order to truly stop police brutality against Black and Brown peoples, if not entirely purge gun-toting officers from minority neighborhoods altogether, America must first acknowledge its ties to a White supremacist, ultra-capitalist, hyper-exploitative system that for over 400 years has reduced Black and Brown folk to property and throwaway things. The longer we delay practical and achievable public policy transformation, the more I dread that schools and communities, of any racial or class background, will fall further into a subdued state of caged existence. While change can be unpleasant for many, recent nationwide protests have made it clear that a social and cultural reckoning is underway, with schools being a major part of this imminent shift.

HRH

Endorsements

Always on Lockdown cuts through the academic discourse on the subject of policing in schools and brings us up-close to the situation of schooling in the age of security and the school-to-prison pipeline. Readers get the views of people who live the experience. There are reflections, questions and resources that make this book an excellent text for teaching. And there are plenty of insights by both the young and the old, the student and the teacher, the parent and the professional, to educate us on a world that is all-too-often invisible and misunderstood.

Ronnie Casella, Associate Dean, School of Education, State University of New York at Cortland and author of At Zero Tolerance: Punishment, Prevention, and School Violence, *and* "Being Down": Challenging Violence in Urban Schools.

The walls of many schools are adorned with slogans about freedom to learn and preparation for democracy; however, actual practice in far too many of those schools is fraught with regulations that thwart liberation of learning and prepare students for autocracy. *Always on*

Lockdown makes this concrete through the seldom heard voices of students, teachers, other school workers, and parents who experience the daily frustration of schooling that often mirrors prison conditions. This book is a tribute to the insights that reside within those who live in *lockdown schools* every day: urban, suburban or rural. It raises awareness of the need to create educational settings that enable the possibilities embodied in students and teachers to unfold, flourish, and imagine a better world.

> *William H. Schubert, Professor Emeritus, former Chair of Curriculum and Instruction, University Scholar at the University of Illinois at Chicago, and author of* Love, Justice, and Education, *and* Curriculum: Perspective, Paradigm, and Possibility.

In *Always on Lockdown*, Dr. Horace Hall gives literal voice to students, parents, principals, counselors and school cops swept up in the convulsive reform known as Renaissance 2010, which shuttered dozens of schools and forced thousands of children and youths into new environments, across neighborhood lines with often chaotic, unsafe results. By documenting the experiences and insights of these Chicago students and their allies, Dr. Hall makes clear that safe learning environments are not constructed with more surveillance cameras and metal detectors. It is a lesson that, sadly, Chicago's political class has only begun to learn.

> *Annette Fuentes, award winning journalist who writes for* The New York Times, The Nation, The Progressive *and* The Village Voice. *She is also the author of* Lockdown High: When the Schoolhouse Becomes a Jailhouse.